# A Time to Bond

*A parent-to-parent guide to making the most of visits with children in foster care*

By Rise
Edited by Nora McCarthy

**Rise**

**EDITOR**
Nora McCarthy

**LAYOUT & DESIGN**
Jeff Faerber

**PROOFREADING**
Rachel Blustain

**COVER ART**
Thaynia Waldron

For reprint information, please contact Rise.

ISBN 978-1-935552-50-5

Printed in the United States of America

Rise®
New York, New York
www.risemagazine.org

# Introduction

*A Time to Bond* is a workbook designed to support and guide parents in making the most of visits with children in foster care. It includes true stories by parents who have successfully reunified with children in foster care, interviews with experts on visiting, and lessons and worksheets for using the stories in a visiting support group for parents. The parent stories explain the purpose of visits and model how parents have solved problems in their visits. The discussion guides and worksheets make it easy for facilitators to help parents understand positive visiting practices, reflect on their own visits, and plan visits that are more fun and more meaningful for their entire family.

Parents at different stages of a child welfare case can benefit from a visiting support group based on *A Time to Bond*. The group can help parents whose children have just entered foster care get off to the right start. The group also can serve as an intervention for parents who are struggling with visits or who have had their visits reduced. Finally, the group can include parents who are succeeding in visits, who can serve as peer role models.

Stories from *A Time to Bond* also can be used in parenting classes or one-on-one discussions with caseworkers or visit supervisors. Parents can arrive early or stay late after a visit to read a story and discuss it with the visit supervisor, caseworker or parent advocate. Parenting class facilitators can use stories and lessons to help participants understand how to best parent their children while their children are in foster care. Agencies that use true stories by parents in their work send the message, "We listen to parents. We respect parents' knowledge. We want parents to succeed."

# CONTENTS

## About Rise

Rise trains parents to write about their experiences with the child welfare system in order to support parents and parent advocacy and guide child welfare practitioners and policymakers in becoming more responsive to the families and communities they serve.

Our print and online magazine reaches parents nationwide. We work with family support and child welfare agencies to use Rise stories in support groups, parent education classes and staff training. We partner with advocacy organizations to use Rise stories in child welfare reform. Learn more about Rise at our website, www.risemagazine.org.

## Acknowledgments

*A Time to Bond* was published with support from the Child Welfare Fund, Annie E. Casey Foundation and New York City Children's Services. Staff at New York City's Children's Services and Children's Aid Society were essential to developing this project. Our deepest appreciation goes to the writers who contributed their stories; to Rise Editorial Board Member Bevanjae Kelley, who helped Rise to improve its workbook format; and to Marty Beyer, whose Visit Coaching method formed a basis for conceptualizing the workbook.

# Leader's Guide: How to run a parent support group with *A Time to Bond*

## *Visiting Support Group Format*

A visiting support group using *A Time to Bond* can last 6-8 weeks and include 8-10 parents.

• On day one, participants read an overview of the purposes of visits and positive visiting strategies, written by a parent advocate at a foster care agency.

• Each week, parents read a story out loud and discuss how the parent writer handled one aspect of visiting: recognizing their children's needs, planning routines and activities to meet their children's needs, keeping parents' negative feelings out of the visit, communicating with foster parents, and communicating with their children.

• Parents complete a worksheet designed to help them reflect on their own visits and set goals.

• The following week, parents share the steps they took to reach their goals during their latest visit.

• In the final session, parents celebrate their achievements, set goals for future visits, and receive a certificate for participation that they can show to their caseworkers, judge and lawyer.

*Six-week group:* You can complete the group in 6 weeks by covering two stories on the first day— "A Time to Bond," and " Winning Him Back," on p. 18 and p. 24. On the last day, you can extend the length of the group and hold a small celebration, asking participants to fill out the worksheet on p. 81 called "My Achievements and Goals" and handing out certificates.

*Eight-week group:* If you have time, you may want to complete the group in 8 weeks. On the first day, read only "A Time to Bond," and give participants plenty of time to discuss their experiences and goals. Use the 8th day to complete the "My Achievements and Goals" worksheet, and to spend time reflecting on and celebrating participants' achievements.

## *Optional Stories*

In addition to the seven stories covered in the curriculum, *A Time to Bond* includes four stories marked "Helping Hand." Two are interviews with experts about using visits to bond with their children: "Standing in Your Child's Shoes" on p. 42 and "Bonding with Baby" on p. 52. If you have extra time during a session, you can ask participants to read the story out loud and ask some basic questions to get a discussion started:

• What's something new that you learned from this story?

• Did anything this expert said surprise you?

• What can you take from this story?

Two stories are by parents who facilitate Visit Hosting or Visit Coaching, model programs for helping parents improve visits. Agencies that offer Visiting Hosting or Coaching can include these stories in the group to familiarize parents with this support. If you would like to recommend that an individual parent seek Visit Hosting or Coaching, you can ask the parent to read the story and discuss it with you one-on-one.

### Recruiting Parent Participants

An ideal group will include parents with a mix of experiences with visiting. Caseworkers may choose to refer parents to the group after intake to get off on the right foot, or because concerns about visits are impeding their progress. Parents may wish to join the group because they are feeling overwhelmed during visits or because their visit frequency has been set back. Or, parents who are progressing in their service plan might join in order to impress upon the judge and caseworker their seriousness about reunification. Parents nearing reunification might join to support other parents.

*Presentations to Staff:* To recruit a good group, you may want to present about the group at a staff meeting so that caseworkers and other staff understand the resource you're offering. If you have time, ask the group to read a sample story out loud. Wanda Chamber's story "Step by Step" on p. 12 is included for use in an open house or staff meeting.

*Open House for Parents:* Create flyers to advertise an open house about the group. A sample flyer is included on p. 11. Hand out the flyers and hang them up.

Hold an open house for parents interested in the group. Ask parents to take turns reading out loud Wanda Chambers' story "Step by Step" on p. 12. Explain *A Time to Bond* and the format of the group. Start the group within a week.

### Including Parents With Limited Literacy:

Parents do not need to be literate or able to read or write well to take part in the visiting support group. When the group is reading a story out loud, the facilitator can call only on parents who feel comfortable reading. Instead of asking participants to fill out the worksheets individually, the facilitator can lead the entire group through the worksheets and write responses on big paper or a white board. Or, if parents are not too uncomfortable with others knowing that they are limited in reading or reading English, parents can go over the worksheet in a pair with another parent.

### Offering a Certificate

A certificate for completion of the group will help parent participants demonstrate to their caseworkers, lawyers and judges that they've taken an additional step to improve their connection to their children. A certificate will motivate parents to join the group and attend regularly.

You may want to set clear standards for certificate completion before the group begins. For instance, you may require participants to arrive on time, participate in all activities, notify the group leader of an absence, complete the discussion questions and worksheets on their own in case of an absence, and miss no more than one class in the cycle. Or, you may want to set qualifications through a group discussion on the first day, asking the group, "What do you think everyone should have to do to earn a certificate?" Regardless of your method, type up the standards for earning a certificate, hand them out, and review them during the first or second group.

Keep track of lateness, attendance, etc., in a public way so that group members are aware if they are jeopardizing their certificate. On the last day, hand out certificates in a celebratory way. To make a certificate, you can buy certificate paper that goes in a printer and type up the text. A sample certificate is provided on p. 14.

### Ending the Group

On the last day, you'll want to celebrate participants' achievements. Have everyone fill out the worksheet "My Achievements and Goals." Ask participants to share their achievements and goals with each other. Take a few moments to share your own observations of growth you've seen in group members.

Hold a small party by serving a meal or cake and handing out certificates. You might want to make this event semi-public by inviting family members or caseworkers.

You may want to play a simple game with participants: Everyone tapes one sheet of paper to their backs and has a (non-permanent) marker. Everyone writes something nice on everyone else's back. It's a mad scramble. Then each person has the chance to read what others wrote about her and can keep the paper.

Finally, if the group has gelled, you may want to encourage participants to exchange contact information so that they can continue to provide peer support to each other once the group is over. Use the worksheet on p. 81 called "My Support Team."

# Running the Group

Each member of the group should receive a copy of *A Time to Bond*. Ideally, parents will bring the workbook back and forth to the group, filling in the Visit Journal reflections at home. If you have concerns about participants arriving prepared, keep their copies of *A Time to Bond* at the office and make photocopies of each week's Visit Journal worksheet for participants to take home and fill out at home.

The Leader's Guides for each story include a basic guideline of everything you'll need to say to run the group. Of course, you can adapt this guideline as you feel comfortable. The guideline is there to help you move from one activity to the next.

• Prepare for the group each week by reading the introduction, story and lesson in advance.

• After week one, each workshop will begin with a discussion of the "My Visit Journal" worksheet from the previous week. Participants should have set a goal for each visit related to the topic discussed in the group. After the visit, they should have filled out the "reflections" questions at home. Begin by asking participants to take out their worksheets called "My Visit Journal."

Start a discussion using the questions at the bottom of the previous lesson marked "next week." (15-20 minutes)

• Then move on to this week's story. Read the day's topic and introduction out loud to the group. (2 minutes)

• Ask participants to take turns reading the story out loud. (10-15 minutes)

• Use the discussion questions to guide a discussion of the story. Keep the discussion focused on the story writer's experiences and strengths. If participants are taking the discussion off course, use the questions to bring the discussion back into focus. (15 minutes)

• Ask parents to fill out the worksheet marked "My Reflections." Once most people seem to be finished, give a 2-minute warning. Then ask everyone to put their pens down and listen to one another. (10 minutes)

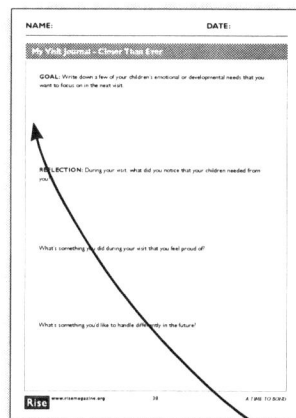

• Ask participants to read their answers out loud, or just talk about their answers. This is where participants really share their own plans, fears, and hopes. Let this discussion extend, and ask little follow-up questions, like, "Can you tell us more about that?" (10-15 minutes)

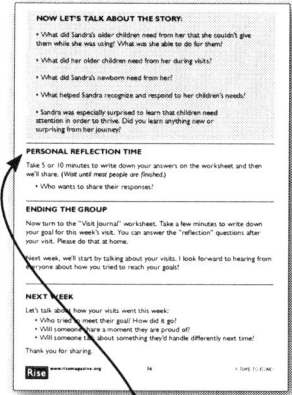

• Ask parents to turn to the worksheet marked "My Visit Journal." Ask everyone to write down one goal, or a few simple goals, for their next visit. Participants should read their goals out loud. (10-15 minutes)

• Parents should complete the "reflections" questions on the "My Visit Journal" worksheet at home, after their next visit. If participants consistently arrive without the reflections questions filled in, give everyone 10 minutes to prepare at the beginning of each group.

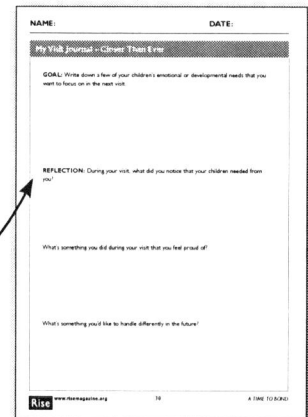

# Group Facilitation Tips

• During the first meeting, ask participants to come up with rules for how everyone will treat each other during the group. This list of rules should be specific, including rules about how to respond to texts or calls during the group, whether it's OK to get up and leave the room, whether it's OK to give advice, etc. You may want to prompt group members about active listening skills by saying, "How can we show each other we're listening? What kinds of body language shows people we're listening and what shows that we're not?" If possible, write the group rules on a big piece of paper that's posted on the wall during every session. Refer to it when participants get off track.

• Encourage participants to speak to each other, not you. Instead of maintaining eye contact with whoever is speaking, look at that person briefly and then look at other people in the group. This will help the speaker make eye contact with other group members. Also, sit next to different group members each time. Better conversations and group cohesion can develop if participants don't focus on talking to and pleasing the facilitator.

• While participants are filling out worksheets, stand up and walk around. Gently ask to see what people are writing and give everyone encouragement. Don't allow participants to opt out on answering the questions.

• If some participants don't speak up during discussions, call on people in a nice way: "Paula, would you like to share?" "Alex, can you tell us about your visit?" "Carly, what activities are you planning to do with your children this week?" However, if there are times that no one responds, don't be afraid of silence. Try to wait for someone else to break the silence, or finally say, "Who is going to jump in?" If someone talks too much, you can say, "I'd like to hear from someone who hasn't spoken much today."

# Do you want help with visits?

# Do you want support from other parents?

# Join a VISITING SUPPORT GROUP for PARENTS

**Every week we'll read a true story by a parent who succeeded in reunifying with children in foster care.**

- Share your experiences and learn from other parents.
- Learn what you can do to improve your visits and get more visits.
- Earn a certificate that you can show to your caseworker, lawyer and judge.

**Learn more about this VISITING SUPPORT GROUP for PARENTS.**

When:

Where:

If you can't attend the meeting, speak with your caseworker or

_____

about how to join the group.

**Rise**

Parent stories are from Rise, a magazine by and for parents affected by the child welfare system. www.risemagazine.org

# Step by Step

*My daughter couldn't stand me when I started visiting.*

By Wanda Chambers

In 1998 I was pregnant with my daughter when I was arrested for possession of crack cocaine. I was given a conditional release to go to a drug treatment program but for a long time I could not get it right.

When Ebony was 6 months old, someone reported me and the child welfare system put her in foster care. Honestly, I felt relieved because I knew I wasn't doing right with Ebony. Once she went into care, I didn't have to worry about whether she was safe.

Eventually, I got locked up. I was sent upstate to Bedford Hills Correctional Facility and by the time I got there I was more alert because I had been clean for months. I said to myself, "I'm going to start communicating with the agency." I grew up in foster care myself so I could relate to my daughter's struggle and, once I was clean, I was committed to getting her out of foster care.

My daughter had been in care a year and a half at that point. I asked for reports and pictures of my daughter, but I never got visits. All I knew was that she was with a Spanish family and I was concerned that she wouldn't speak English. She was 3 years old when I saw her again.

### Slowly Reconnecting

When I began visiting my daughter, she couldn't stand my living guts. Ebony was afraid of me and was really not nice. She wouldn't talk to me. She'd scream when I got near her. She'd sit under the desk for the whole visit, or keep running out in the hall to see her foster mother. I would keep reading, "And the bear said…" and if she looked at me I'd say, "Hello, Ebony." Of course I went home and cried.

At first, the foster mother and I did not get along. I felt that the foster mother's presence during visits was making it harder for me and my daughter to bond. My daughter kept going out in the hall to talk with her foster mother and it made me crazy. I said, "I'm going to ask them to remove the foster mother from the agency during the time of my visit."
She fought me tooth and nail, one mother fighting another mother. She would say my daughter acted out after visits and she blamed me.

## Step by Step

Still, I went step by step—I kept working on my relationship with Ebony and went from supervised to community visits to weekends. Ebony and I got closer when I was able to take her out to the park and then, when we had weekend visits, I could do little things like wipe her face and do her hair and put on her shoes. When I could sleep with her next to me I felt really connected with her. I'm very emotional, and when her little hand would touch my leg, it would send chills through my body.

As my daughter's foster mother realized that my daughter was really on her way home, she began to be a friend to me.

## 'We Can All Live Together'

The day my daughter came home for good, I felt like I should give Ebony back to the foster family because they loved her so much and she loved them. We'd had overnights, but it was nothing to prepare any of us for what felt like the final goodbye.

That day, the whole foster family brought her to my door. They pulled up in a minivan with about 15 Spanish people in it, brothers and sisters, all crying—crying on the floor, crying in the street, taking all of her belongings out of the car, screaming, "My princess, my baby."

I was planning to end their relationship with my daughter. I wanted her home with me, period. But later on, when I was bathing my daughter, she said to me, "This is what we can do. We can put your house and their house together and we can all live together." My heart went out to Ebony. I'm a woman of compassion, and I told myself, "There is no way I'm going end this relationship. I can't do that to

them or to her."

## A Loving Connection

In the months after my daughter came home, her foster family continued to show love to us both. I called her foster mother once and said, "Why isn't this child eating?" We realized that Ebony was used to the Spanish food and I cook black people food. So her foster mom would bring pans and pans of food. She taught me to cook pastelitos and peas and rice.

Today my daughter is 10 and she is an amazing little girl. My daughter's former foster mother is still part of our lives. Ebony stays with her in the summers and she often babysits since I'm working and going to school.

I'm working as a parent advocate at the Brooklyn Family Defense Project, which represents parents in court and supports parents by assigning a lawyer, social worker and parent advocate to each case. I tell the parents my story. I pull out my dispositions and my certificates and say, "You can sit on this side of the desk if you do what you need to do."

---

**Let's talk about this story:**

• **What motivated Wanda to want to visit her daughter?**

• **When she began visiting, what obstacles did she face?**

• **What steps did Wanda take to improve visits with her daughter?**

• **What can we learn from Wanda's experience?**

Rise

# Certificate of Achievement

## Congratulations!

This certifies that

_____

successfully completed a Parent Support Group focused on
making the most of visits with children in foster care

from _____ to _____

at _____

Group facilitator _____

Contact: _____

Signature: _____

# LEADER'S GUIDE: Day One

## WELCOMING THE GROUP

Thank you everyone for coming to this group. This is a group about visits with children in foster care. We hope it will give you a chance to understand what's expected of you in visits, to reflect on your visits, and to learn from other parents.

Each week, we are going to read a story by a parent about her experience visiting her children in foster care. The stories were written by real parents who have reunified with their children. They were written for *Rise*, a magazine by and for parents affected by the child welfare system. The stories show how parents like yourselves were able to deal with the challenges of visits and move their families toward reunification.

Each story in the workbook comes with worksheets to help you reflect in writing on your own experiences with visits and set goals for your visits. Each week, after we read about how another parent overcame a challenge she was facing in her visits, we'll take some time to talk and think together about the steps each of you can take to handle similar challenges.

## PRIVACY

The expectation is that you will try new things during visits to make visits a better experience for you and your children. Not everything you try is going to work out perfectly the first time. That's OK. Keep trying. You're not going to be judged in this group.

I am not going to talk with anyone involved in your case about the struggles you may share in this group, unless you say something that shows that you're at risk of harming someone else or yourself. Everyone in the group should keep our discussions private. This is a private place to talk and reflect on your visits, to try new things, and to grow as a parent.

Do you have any questions about sharing with the group?

## SELF-INTRODUCTIONS

Before we begin, let's go around and introduce ourselves. Can everyone say a little bit about why you are here today? You can just say your name and:
• a little bit about your children
• their names and ages
• what led you to join this group
Who wants to start?

Thank you for sharing a little bit about yourselves.

## RULES + EXPECTATIONS

Before we begin reading our first story, I want to let you know some basic information about the group:

First, we're going to meet from _____ to _____ *(hours)* every _____ *(day of the week).*

During the group, there are some rules that everyone will have to follow so that we can learn from each other. *[Hand out a sheet explaining basic rules or ask the group to define group standards.]*

You can earn a certificate for completing the group if you come regularly and on time, and you participate. *[Hand out a sheet explaining the attendance rules or ask the group to define the standards for a certificate.]*

Do any of you have questions about the rules or about the group itself?

## READING AND DISCUSSING STORIES

In our group, we're going to read all of the stories out loud. If you feel comfortable reading out loud, please read a section or two. If you don't feel comfortable, that's OK. Remember, everyone makes mistakes when they read out loud. Let's not worry too much about mistakes.

Does anyone have questions about reading out loud? Great, let's begin.

## LEADER'S GUIDE:

**A Time to Bond** by Jacquelyn Israel
Making the most of your visits.

---

## TODAY WE'LL TALK ABOUT:
**What you want to work on in your visits**

---

### INTRODUCTION

Today we'll read a story that gives you a basic overview of what is expected of you in visits and what you can do to make your family time as positive as possible. The story was written by Jacquelyn Israel. Her own children were in foster care for three years. After they came home, she started working as a Parent Advocate at a foster care agency.

The story combines what Jacquelyn learned when she was visiting her own children, and what she's learned from supervising visits and helping parents improve their visits. Unlike other stories that we'll read, it gives advice. It explains very clearly how different actions during visits may help or hurt you.

Let's read Jacquelyn's story and talk about what all of you are doing well during visits and what you want to work on during this group.

---

### READ AND DISCUSS STORY

Let's take turns reading the story out loud. Who wants to start?

# A Time To Bond

*Making the most of your visits.*

By Jacquelyn Israel

*Jacquelyn Israel, whose children spent six years in foster care, is a parent advocate at Graham Windham. She helps parents at the agency understand their rights and get the help they need. Here she explains how to make the most of your visits.*

### 1. Bring Toys and Games

When you visit at the agency, the room just isn't a home environment. I suggest that parents bring games, coloring books, activity books, crayons. Play some soft music, and bring books to read to your child. You can even bring your own visiting blanket so you and your children can sit down on the floor with Legos and blocks.

### 2. Make Visits a Time to Bond

During the visit, you definitely want to interact. Sometimes I see parents come and they look at the kid, sitting far apart. It's not like visiting at a hospital. It's a time to strengthen the bond you have with your child.

Some parents want to do homework with the children, and it's a good thing to care about your child's education, but if homework is troubling and causes tension in your family, I wouldn't suggest doing that during a visit. When you're getting frustrated, you're not building your bond.

Don't use your visits to complain about the situation, or dump your feelings on your child. That takes quality time away from your child.

### 3. Don't Make Promises You Can't Keep

One of the hardest moments is when children ask, "When am I coming home?" Be as truthful and honest as you can be, while keeping in mind the child's age. Tell your children, "I wish I could take you home right now, but I can't. I'm working on it, and I'll take you home as soon as possible."

Don't make promises that you can't keep. If you say, "You'll be home next week," and it doesn't happen, your child won't know who to trust, or what is true and what is false.

### 4. Expect Your Kids to Act Up

It's normal for a child to feel angry or scared about being in foster care, and to act up as a result. When parents hear that a child is acting up, they start thinking, "Why is this happening? Is someone hurting my child." They feel powerless.

You might feel very scared if you feel you can't help your child. You might even start acting out, becoming angry or explosive. But you can help your children by reassuring them that you're working to get them home, and letting them know that you love them and care about them

Rise

even when you're not together.

You also want to let your child know that there's nothing they can do to get home faster. I've seen children act out because they believe that if they act bad, the system will say, "This child is too bad, we better send the child home to their mom."

## 5. Build a Relationship with the Foster Mom

You can help your child and your case by being polite to the foster parent. At visits, say, "Hello. How are my kids? How are they in school? Can I meet you for open school night?"

To get your children back, you have to be part of your child's life, and the foster mom can help you with that. It's good if the foster mom can say in court, "I met the children's mother at the children's doctor's appointment," or, "For open school night we met and went together to discuss the children's education."

When my kids were in care, the court could say to me, "Jacqueline, you were a bad parent for all these things you did in the past." But I could say, "I have a relationship with my children that's nurturing, structured and not damaging." And the foster mom supported me in saying that.

## 6. Help Your Children Say Goodbye

Parents and their children don't want visits to end. Children have a hard time because they don't understand why they can't go home. They cry, have fits.

Don't prolong the visit. Help your children say goodbye, and let them know you'll see them soon. When it's almost time to leave, help your child get ready to go. Say, "It's time for us to go now. Please take care. I'll see you soon. Ask the foster parent if you can call me." Say goodbye and leave your child with the foster parent.

I see some parents who stay with their children as long as they can. One parent follows the foster parent's car. Don't do that. That's not a healthy thing for the children to see. If you break the rules, your children get the idea that they can also choose whether to follow rules. That will hurt your children in school and when they come back home.

## 7. Keep Visiting and It Will Get Easier

Sometimes I hear parents say, "It's just too hard to visit my child at the agency." But the agency is not going to say, "Take all the time you need and your child will be there for you when you're ready." You need to prove to the agency that you care about your child.

You and your child will feel better if you spend more time together. Even a week apart can feel like an eternity to a child, because children are having new experiences every day. One month they're in diapers. Soon they're saying, "You mean to tell me that light has a speed and water turns into clouds?"

Do your best to bond with your child, and the visits will get easier.

## NOW LET'S TALK ABOUT THE STORY:

• Which of Jacquelyn's suggestions do you think you're already doing in visits with your children?

• Did any of Jacquelyn's suggestions surprise you? Are there some you haven't done before? Or that you're having trouble with?

• Jacquelyn describes how parents can feel powerless, overwhelmed, angry and sad during visits. How does she suggest dealing with these difficult emotions?

## PERSONAL REFLECTION TIME

Let's look at the worksheet called "My Reflections." Take 5 or 10 minutes to write down your answers on the first worksheet, and then we'll share. (*Wait until most people are finished.*)
  • Who wants to share what they wrote for the first question—what's going well in your visits?
  • Who wants to share their concerns?
  • What do you want to get out of this group?

## ENDING THE GROUP

Now turn to the "Visit Journal" worksheet. Take a few minutes to write down your goal for this week's visit. You can answer the "reflection" questions after your visit. Please do that at home.

Next week, we'll start by talking about your visits. I look forward to hearing from everyone about how you tried to reach your goals!

## NEXT WEEK

Let's talk about how your visits went this week:
  • Who tried to meet their goal? How did it go?
  • Will someone share a moment they are proud of?
  • Will someone talk about something they'd handle differently next time?
Thank you for sharing.

## My Reflections: A Time to Bond by Jacquelyn Israel

1. What is going well during visits with your children?

2. What concerns do you have about your family visits?

3. What do you want to learn about in this group?

4. What are your goals for your visits?

## My Visit Journal – A Time to Bond

**GOAL:** Use your next visit to pay attention to what's going well during visits and what you want to work on over the next six weeks.

**REFLECTION:** What's something you did during your visit that you feel proud of?

What's something you'd like to handle differently in the future?

What help do you feel you need to improve your visits?

## LEADER'S GUIDE:

**Winning Him Back** by Lynne Miller
My visits proved I was worth my son's trust.

---

## TODAY WE'RE GOING TO TALK ABOUT:
How you can prove that you can be trusted

---

### INTRODUCTION

When children enter foster care, they lose trust that their parents can keep them safe. Your visits are a time to show your children that they can count on you. You can show them that they can trust you to arrive at visits on time, come to every visit, and come prepared with toys, games and snacks. Most of all, you can show your children that you've come ready to play with them, listen to them, and enjoy your family time.

Visiting children in foster care can be stressful, sad and confusing. Your children may look or act differently during visits than they did at home. Just being at the agency or seeing your child's foster parent can stir up negative feelings.

Despite these challenges, you must visit as scheduled and use your visit to show your children and the agency staff that they can trust you. You will be judged on how prepared you are for visits, how you treat your child's foster parent, and how you treat your children. Your visits will affect how quickly your children return home. Let's read Lynne's story and talk about how you can prove that you're trustworthy.

---

### READ AND DISCUSS STORY

Let's take turns reading the story out loud. Who wants to start?

# Winning Him Back

*My visits proved I was worth my son's trust.*

By Lynne Miller

My baby's father passed away when I was pregnant. After, I felt I had to block out everything I was feeling so I wouldn't lose the baby. But I found out later that those feelings were still with me.

For three years, life was pretty uneventful for my son and me. We went to the park to feed the squirrels. We watched Sesame Street and Barney together. He would help me make dinner and we'd eat it together. We spent a lot of time just the two of us.

## Black Hole Inside Me
Then my mother died and a black hole opened up inside me. All the feelings I'd held back for so long came rushing back. I didn't want to feel those feelings so I started snorting cocaine and smoking crack, too.

Soon, my son and I were spending a lot less time together. I'd send him to his room by himself to watch TV for hours. He'd even eat in front of the television by himself.

The next year, ACS took him away from me. I never thought I'd get him back. My ACS worker told me that she would make sure the foster parents he was with would adopt him right out of my life. She said there wasn't a thing I could do about it—and I believed her!

I felt like my world had ended.

## 'Is This My Son?'
The first time I was able to see my son was about six weeks after they took him. When the agency sent me a letter to let me know where my son was living, I was overjoyed—and scared. I didn't know what to expect or how to act.

I was a nervous wreck on the bus ride to go see him. And when he arrived at the agency where I was impatiently waiting, I didn't recognize him. When they took him from me, he had a long tail and hair to just above his collar. Now his hair was shaved in sort of a mushroom cut.

When I was told, "There's your son," I think I went into shock, and my son and I spent nearly the whole visit crying all over each other.

Maybe it was the guilt I was feeling, but I felt I could see the mistrust in my son's eyes. I didn't know how I would be able to win back the trust I had stupidly forfeited.

### He Called Someone Else 'Mom'

The worst part of the visit was when I heard him call the foster mother "mom." I flipped out. After the worker and foster mom calmed me down, they explained to me that it was to make him feel at ease, and because her other foster kids called her that too.

They tried to reassure me that I still was and would always be his mom. But here was my son calling some other lady "Mom." I felt sure this was just another proof that my ACS worker was making good her threat to keep my child from me. Then she told me it would be two weeks before I would be able to see my son again, and that would be only for one hour. I was devastated. I left there in a daze.

### Starting the Healing Process

Seeing my son for one hour every two weeks took a toll on our relationship. I felt like I was in a bad dream that I was moving through in slow motion. I no longer knew how to act or what to say around him. The worst part was saying good-bye after every visit. That's when all the guilt and remorse really set in. I wanted to kick myself for being such a screw-up.

I think my showing up consistently for our visits started the healing process. It helped to show my son that I could be trusted again. If I told him I would be at the agency to see him in two weeks, and then I showed up, he knew I was reliable and kept my word. It also showed the agency that I was capable of being a responsible

parent again.

I also began coming to a focus group for biological parents to ask questions and get information. I ended up helping to organize their Birth Parent Advocates Program. That support helped me manage the hard times.

### His Foster Mom Supported Me

As I came to know my son's foster mother, she made our visits go easier and helped me get my son back. My agency, Seamen's Society for Children and Families, has a family-to-family approach—that is, we try to keep open communication between the birth and foster parents so that a friendship can develop.

This lets the children know they aren't a prize being competed for; they are loved and cared for and have just acquired an "extended family" to help take care of them while their birth parents are unable.

My son's foster mom would assure my son that he'd be going home someday soon. She even had the agency's psych department give my son therapy to help him with all the new and confusing feelings he was having.

### Little Adjustments

The only problem I had with my son's foster mom was that I felt my son was being spoiled. At every visit, he had a new toy or a new outfit to show me. I didn't know how I was going to keep that up once I got him back. Soon I was bringing him presents, too.

When I spoke to the foster mom about the presents, she said that she understood and scaled back on what she got him (or at least what I saw of it).

I also stopped bringing anything but food to visits, except on special occasions. I wanted to be sure my son was happy to see *me*. I wanted our visits to be about us, not about me sitting and watching him play with his new toy.

At first I didn't ask my son too much about where he was living. I didn't want to hear that they were taking better care of him than I had when I was using drugs. But after a while I did ask. My son told me he liked having a lot of kids to play with, that the house was really nice and that he had pets to take care of. I was very jealous. At the time, I didn't believe I'd ever be able to provide a good home for him again.

### My Son Comes Home

Eventually, our visits were increased to one hour once a week, and then two hours every week. Finally, I was able to take him for an occasional overnight, then weekends. Having my child over night again created new tensions and stresses for both of us. He wasn't real sure how to act with me; I worried about saying the wrong thing or losing my cool. But I just took it minute by minute, and eventually we began to have a natural relationship again.

You can't know how wonderful it is to be able to just call your child in from the backyard to eat dinner until you've experienced not having him there to call. I found most pleasure in the smallest things; wiping away a tear, kissing a booboo or just getting a hug.

The best Christmas present I've ever gotten was when I was told I could have my son for his Christmas vacation from school. That became his trial discharge home to me. After almost 18 months of hard work, I got him back!

### Ups and Downs

My son has been home almost three years. We still have our ups and downs. One consistent thing has been our relationship with his former foster parents. My son has spent many nights and weekends at their house. He's gone with them on vacations and to family celebrations, ball games, swim meets and more. I have gone to some, too!

Packing up my son for a vacation or overnight, I've felt grateful that my son has had another family that enriches his life. I also feel good that I'm no longer an angry, jealous and resentful person but one who can appreciate that my son benefits from the caring of a family that took him into their hearts and home.

My son still occasionally acts out in school and every once in a while he has a bad nightmare, like he did after he was taken away from me. I am in the process of trying to find a therapist for him that I can afford. I think it's important because the feelings he experienced while I was using drugs and then when he was in foster care aren't going to disappear just because we're a family again. My son and I talk to each other about what happened and how I hope he believes me when I tell him it will never happen again.

## NOW LET'S TALK ABOUT THE STORY:

• How did Lynne earn her son's trust?

• How did she win the agency's trust?

• How did she win the foster mother's trust?

• What challenges did Lynne face?

• How did she resolve them?

## PERSONAL REFLECTION TIME

Let's turn to the worksheet called "My Reflections." Take 5 or 10 minutes to write down your answers on the worksheet and then we'll share. (*Wait until most people are finished.*)

• What are some things you're doing well? Who wants to share their responses?

• What are some things you're not doing or need help to do better?

## ENDING THE GROUP

Now turn to the "Visit Journal" worksheet. Take a few minutes to write down your goal for this week's visit. You can answer the "reflection" questions and fill in the checklist after your visit. Please do that at home.

Next week, we'll start by talking about your visits. I look forward to hearing from everyone about how you tried to reach your goals!

## NEXT WEEK

Let's talk about how your visits went this week:
• Who tried to meet their goal? How did it go?
• Will someone share a moment they are proud of?
• Will someone talk about something they'd handle differently next time?
Thank you for sharing.

**NAME:** _____        **DATE:** _____

## My Reflections: Winning Him Back by Lynne Miller

In Lynne's story, we see her take many steps to prove to the agency and to her son that she is trustworthy and capable of caring for her child. Take a moment to reflect on how you're doing with each step Lynne took:

| What Lynne Does | How I'm Doing |
|---|---|
| • Attends all visits | |
| • Arrives on time | |
| • Brings snack | |
| • Greets foster parent | |
| • Resolves conflict with foster parent | |
| • Focuses only on child in visit | |
| • Tries to keep anger out of visit | |
| • Finds support for herself | |
| • Responds to her child's needs: | |
|    —for Mom to be trustworthy | |
|    —to have fun with Mom | |
|    —to eat together | |
|    —to feel safe with foster parent | |
|    —to talk about his experiences | |

## My Visit Journal – Winning Him Back

**GOAL:** Based on today's discussion, what is one thing you want to do differently during your next visit?

**REFLECTION:** Did you try to reach your goal during your visit this week? How did it go?

What's something you did during your visit that you feel proud of?

What's something you'd like to handle differently in the future?

OVER ————————→

## My Visit Journal Checklist: Winning Him Back by Lynne Miller

Please use the checklist below to keep track of the steps you are taking to improve your visits. Use the "comments" section to make notes about your experiences.

| Did I... | Comments |
|---|---|
| ☐ Attend my visit | |
| ☐ Arrive on time | |
| ☐ Plan activities | |
| ☐ Bring toys | |
| ☐ Bring a snack | |
| ☐ Greet my child's foster parent | |
| ☐ Keep anger/frustration out of my visit | |
| ☐ Focus only on my child | |

Did I respond to my child's needs...

| | |
|---|---|
| ☐ for me to be trustworthy | |
| ☐ to follow a routine | |
| ☐ to have fun together | |
| ☐ to eat together | |
| ☐ to feel safe with the foster parent | |
| ☐ to talk about experiences in foster care | |
| ☐ to say goodbye in a positive way | |

# LEADER'S GUIDE:

**Closer Than Ever** by Sandra Evans
I'm learning how to handle my children without getting high.

---

## TODAY WE'LL TALK ABOUT:
**Thinking about your child's needs during visits**

---

### INTRODUCTION

The most important thing for parents to do during visits is to try to step into their children's shoes. Imagine what it is like for your children to have left behind everything familiar and to visit you in a strange place. In foster care, your child is eating different foods, playing with different toys, living by different rules. Your child may be feeling so many mixed up emotions: confusion, sadness, fear, frustration, betrayal, and anger.

What does your child need from you during visits? All children want their parents to listen to them, hug them, play with them, talk with them, and help them deal with the sadness of saying goodbye.

You may not be sure how to meet your child's needs, especially during visits at an agency visit room. Let's read Sandra's story and think about how you can come to understand your children's needs and build a bond during visits.

---

### READ AND DISCUSS STORY

Let's take turns reading the story out loud. Who wants to start?

# Closer Than Ever

*I'm learning how to handle my children without getting high.*

By Sandra Evans

When I was 12, drugs became my way to numb out all the ugly feelings I had inside from being molested and being ignored by my mother, who always put men ahead of her children. Eventually I tried meth and became addicted. Those painful childhood memories, the ones that no one talks about, disappeared with meth.

My addiction escalated when I was about 25 and caring for my four children under age 5. My husband, Francisco, and I lived in a neighborhood where at every fourth house they either used meth or sold it. Soon getting high became my escape from the smallest things—my baby crying, or a fight with Francisco.

## Totally Numb

I'm not sure what triggered me to start using so much. Thinking back, I see it may have been a number of things. Francisco was going to school, which left me home alone all day. I found caring for all of our children overwhelming and was jealous that Francisco was bettering his life. My role as a mother seemed insignificant.

I feared that I did not know how to be a mom. I did some things well. I always made sure my children were fed and bathed. We would read together and go to the park by our house. But I was really stressed out because I was afraid of making all the mistakes that my mother had made with me.

My addiction made my parenting worse. I was always frustrated with my children and Francisco. I would yell at my oldest, who was only 5, "Make Emiliano a bottle" or, "Take care of your brothers." Other times I did what I had to do but with no emotion. I had become totally numb.

When I got pregnant again, I knew I needed to quit and I wanted to. I would tell myself, "This hit will be the last," but I kept using.

## No More Hiding

Francisco knew I had used meth socially, but I hid my addiction from him. Then we went to the hospital because I felt like I was going into labor. I hadn't gotten prenatal care and didn't know how far along I was, so the doctor did all sorts of tests. He told us that I had tested positive for meth.

I told Francisco, "There is no way. I haven't touched the stuff."

He just gave me a look of disappointment and said, "Babe, tell me, have you been smoking your stuff?"

I lied again.

"If you are, then you really don't care about me or the kids. And what about the baby you're carrying? If you test positive when you have her, we can lose all of our kids."

## Ashamed and Desperate
The next night, I had bad contractions. I kept telling myself that I could make them stop. I was hoping for more time. But I gave birth that night.

At the hospital, child protective services (CPS) showed up and told us we couldn't take the baby home. I felt ashamed and desperate. I had failed my family and myself. I feared that I would lose my children forever.

That day, I went to the nursery to hold my daughter, who was no longer allowed in my room. I just looked at her, feeling like I was the worst mother in the world. I had jeopardized my whole family, and for what?

## Feeling Betrayed
That day, we went to a meeting at the CPS office. The workers helped Francisco understand how meth affects people and they suggested that I go to an outpatient treatment program so I could be with my family while I got help. But Francisco insisted I go to in-patient outside of our neighborhood, where he knew I would have

an easier time breaking my habit.

I felt betrayed. I felt that he hated me. It really pissed me off that we were in a room full of people passing judgment on me, and I felt like I was a terrible mom, and my husband wasn't backing me up. I felt it was Francisco's job to protect me, even if that meant lying. I now realize that he was looking out for the welfare of our children and for me.

## A Little Bit of Hope
Soon I was admitted to Westlake, where I stayed with my newborn daughter for six months.

The day I was admitted, I felt angry at myself, scared and guilty. I thought, "How did I let it get this far?" But I was still not ready to face reality. In my addiction, I had started to make a lot of empty promises, and even on the day I went to my program, I told my oldest son that I would be home in time to pick him up from school. I could picture the look on my little boys' faces when Daddy went home that night and Mommy wasn't with him. I had let them down again.

Still, I felt hopeful. Maybe, just maybe, if I gave this place a try, they could help me deal with all the raw emotions I carried inside. Then I could go home to my children a better mom.

## I Found Support
In treatment, I met a lot of women that I could relate to. We connected because we'd been through similar experiences.

My counselor, Sharon, also helped me so much. Sharon was a tough woman who didn't listen to any excuses. From the instant she looked at me, I felt that she got me. The loneliness that I had felt for so long began to lift in her presence.

Many times I went to Sharon's office a mess, crying. She'd look at me and tell me, "It's OK, we can fix it. Nothing is engraved in stone." I learned to take one day at a time.

### Rebuilding My Family
Through treatment, I got to connect with my family in a much different way than I had when I was high. Francisco and our children came to visit on Saturdays. I looked forward to our visits. I wanted to hear about everything they had been doing.

I would play with our kids, read to them, color and really enjoy our time. These were things I hadn't done with my children before.

Being in the program with my daughter was a wonderful experience, too. I was able to enjoy taking care of her. We had a special class called Therapeutic Childcare that gave us time and support to bond with our babies.

### Attention and Consistency
The teacher, Ms. V., taught us little things that can set the foundation to connect with your children. For instance, I used to make a bottle, put my baby in the bed, prop up the bottle with a blanket, and that was that. She told me that propping the bottle can make a baby choke, get ear infections, and have trouble learning to stop eating when she is full. Most important, feeding the baby in your arms is a way you show the baby you love and care about her.

I learned that children thrive when they have a daily schedule and when you're consistent with them. Ms. V. told me that it's important to get up early with my children, get them dressed and eat breakfast together. She also reminded me to hold my children, tell them I love them, praise them when they do something good, and stick with a punishment once I have set it.

The most valuable thing I learned was that I needed to set aside time to spend with my children to give them the attention they craved. I didn't realize that children need attention in order to thrive.

Ms. V. gave me confidence that, despite my childhood, I could raise my children without neglecting them. I tried what she suggested and found that her guidance helped me build a stronger connection with all of my children.

### Closer Than Ever
Francisco and I reconnected during Family Group, where we could vent in a productive manner. One-on-one sessions with Sharon helped us to understand the roles we had played in each other's lives and work out our differences without blame.

One Saturday near the end of my treatment, Francisco picked me up to take our children to the zoo. I was thrilled. I had always wanted to do that. I'll never forget the expressions on our children's faces while they looked at the animals. It felt incredible to me that we could experience such joy as a family.

Francisco grabbed my hand and looked at me and said, "I love you, babe." On that day, I knew we were going to be OK. Even though I could not undo the past, we still had a future.

### 'Can I Do It?'
The day I returned home, I was overfilled with joy but also terrified. So many thoughts went through my head, like, "What if I can't do it? What if my kids hate me? Am I going to be able to handle the stress without getting high?"

I had spent six months with only my daughter and in the safe, structured environment of the program. I feared that I wasn't ready for the real world.

A big moment for me came about a month after I returned home. My caseworker, Geneva Thomas, came by for our weekly visit and my 4 year old started acting up. First he threw a ball at her. Immediately, I got on him and told him to stand in the corner. He told me no and continued to throw things.

I knew he was just trying to get attention, so I decided to ignore him. But Geneva saw that I was getting frustrated. "You need to deal with him," she said.

### A Sober Mom
I picked my son up and told him to stand in the corner. He started to shout. Then I was so embarrassed. I wanted to yell at him, "What the hell is wrong with you? Why are you acting like this?"

But that was the old me. I told myself, "That isn't the kind of parent you want to be." So I sat down with him in the corner. I told him we were going to sit there until we calmed down.

It felt like a good solution to me, but Geneva explained that I was punishing myself by sitting there with him. I felt so frustrated and confused. How was I supposed to handle him? Even though it took a lot of work, I finally got my son to stand in time-out by himself.

In the past, moments like this would have overwhelmed me and I would've gotten high. Not this time, though. I'm learning to be a sober mom.

### Handling My Children
Now it's been 18 months since I came home from treatment. I feel good. I know how to build a foundation for my children. I am learning to handle their outbursts in a positive way and am reaching out to Francisco for support.

I'm so glad my social worker didn't just throw me out into the world when I was done with treatment. She stood by me while I got adjusted. She also helped my family move into a new apartment and gave us referrals for furniture, clothing and food. Even after my case was closed, she was there if I had a problem or question.

Now, through a program called Exceptional Parents Unlimited, a child development expert comes and works with my children and me once a week. She brings games for the kids to play or comes up with projects for us to do together, like baking or making our own Christmas ornaments. It helps to strengthen the bond between my children and me.

Francisco and I are also closer than ever. We are able to communicate without fighting. I feel that we can make it through everything and our love will not fade.

## NOW LET'S TALK ABOUT THE STORY:

• What did Sandra's older children need from her that she was able to give them while she was using? What couldn't she do for them?

• What did her older children need from her during visits?

• What did Sandra's newborn need from her?

• What helped Sandra recognize and respond to her children's needs?

• Sandra was especially surprised to learn that children need attention in order to thrive. Did you learn anything new or surprising from her journey?

## PERSONAL REFLECTION TIME

Let's turn to the worksheet called "My Reflections." Take 5 or 10 minutes to write down your answers on the worksheet and then we'll share. (*Wait until most people are finished.*)
   • Who wants to share their responses?

## ENDING THE GROUP

Now turn to the "Visit Journal" worksheet. Take a few minutes to write down your goal for this week's visit. You can answer the "reflection" questions and fill in the checklist after your visit. Please do that at home.

Next week, we'll start by talking about your visits. I look forward to hearing from everyone about how you tried to reach your goals!

## NEXT WEEK

Let's talk about how your visits went this week:
   • Who tried to meet their goal? How did it go?
   • Will someone share a moment they are proud of?
   • Will someone talk about something they'd handle differently next time?

Thank you for sharing.

## My Reflections: Closer Than Ever by Sandra Evans

1. What did your children need from you before entering foster care? What were you able to do for them and what needs couldn't you meet?

2. Children of different ages and stages of development need different things. What ages are your children now and what are the developmental tasks that they're learning right now? (For instance, learning to talk, learning to recognize letters or read, learning to make friends, etc. You can look at the Ages + Stages chart on page 39)

Child's Name: _____ Age: _____
Needs:

1) _____

2) _____

3) _____


Child's Name: _____ Age: _____
Needs:

1) _____

2) _____

3) _____


Child's Name: _____ Age: _____
Needs:

1) _____

2) _____

3) _____

## My Visit Journal – Closer Than Ever

**GOAL:** Write down a few of your children's emotional or developmental needs that you want to focus on in the next visit.

**REFLECTION:** Stepping into your children's shoes during the visit, what did you notice that your children needed from you?

What's something you did during your visit that you feel proud of?

What's something you'd like to handle differently in the future?

OVER ————————→

## My Visit Journal Checklist: Closer Than Ever by Sandra Evans

Please use the checklist below to keep track of the steps you are taking to improve your visits. Use the "comments" section to make notes about your experiences.

| Did I... | Comments |
|---|---|
| ☐ Attend my visit | |
| ☐ Arrive on time | |
| ☐ Plan activities | |
| ☐ Bring toys | |
| ☐ Bring a snack | |
| ☐ Greet my child's foster parent | |
| ☐ Keep anger/frustration out of my visit | |
| ☐ Focus only on my child | |
| Did I respond to my child's needs... | |
| ☐ for me to be trustworthy | |
| ☐ to follow a routine | |
| ☐ to have fun together | |
| ☐ to eat together | |
| ☐ to feel safe with the foster parent | |
| ☐ to talk about experiences in foster care | |
| ☐ to say goodbye in a positive way | |

# Ages and Stages

*Developmental milestones help you know how your child is doing.*

### 3 Months

At three months of age, most babies:

—turn their heads toward bright colors and lights
—move both eyes in the same direction together
—recognize bottle or breast
—respond to their mother's voice
—make cooing sounds
—bring their hands together
—wiggle and kick with arms and legs
—lift head when on stomach
—become quiet in response to sound, especially speech
—smile

### 6 Months

At six months of age, most babies:

—follow moving objects with their eyes
—turn toward the source of normal sound
—reach for objects and pick them up
—switch toys from one hand to the other
—play with their toes
—help hold the bottle during feeding
—recognize familiar faces
—imitate speech sounds
—respond to soft sounds, especially talking
—roll over

### 12 Months

At 12 months of age, most babies:

—get to a sitting position
—pull to a standing position
—stand briefly without support
—crawl
—imitate adults using a cup or telephone
—play peek-a-boo and patty cake
—wave bye-bye
—put objects in a container
—say at least one word
—make "ma-ma" or "da-da" sounds

### 1½ Years

At 1½ years of age, most children:

—like to push and pull objects
—say at least 6 words
—follow simple directions ("Bring the ball")
—pull off shoes, socks and mittens
—can point to a picture that you name in a book
—feed themselves
—make marks on a paper with crayons
—walk without help
—walk backwards
—point, make sounds or try to use words to ask for things
—say "no," shake their head or push away things they don't want

### 2 Years

At two years of age, most children:

—use two-to-three word sentences
—say about 50 words
—recognize familiar pictures
—kick a ball forward
—feed themselves with a spoon
—demand a lot of your attention
—turn 2-3 pages at a time
—like to imitate their parent
—identify hair, eyes, ears and nose by pointing
—build a tower of four blocks
—show affection

### 3 Years

At three years of age, most children:

—throw a ball overhand
—ride a tricycle
—put on their shoes
—open the door
—turn one page at a time
—play with other children for a few minutes
—repeat common rhymes
—use three-to-five-word sentences
—name at least one color correctly

# Standing in Your Child's Shoes

*How to meet your child's needs during visits.*

*Visit Coaching supports parents in planning fun visits that help them bond with their children. Here, Marty Beyer, who developed Visit Coaching, explains how parents can make the most of family time while their children are in foster care:*

One of the most important things for a parent to do during visits is to stand in the child's shoes. Imagine what it's like for your child to be separated from you and to come to the visit, whether they're 2 years old or they're 12 years old. Standing in their shoes, try to imagine: What does my child want from me during our family time?

My child needs me to be fully welcoming. My child needs my full attention in the visit. My child needs praise. My child needs a little "just you, just me" time when we are together. My child needs reassurance. My child needs me to talk about the next time we see each other. My child needs a good ending to the visit.

It's often harder to see emotional needs than physical needs. We know to change a wet diaper or to feed our children. But these emotional needs are just as important as feeding a sandwich to your hungry kid.

### Confusing Feelings
At times, it can be difficult to understand the child's needs. A child might run to a toy as soon as she enters the visit room and not say hello to the parent. Some foster parents or caseworkers might assume that past abuse has made the child afraid of the parent. Actually, it might just be that the child is full of confused feelings during the visit.

Coming in to a visit is difficult for children. Unfortunately, children usually can't explain their feelings. A child won't walk in and say, "I'm feeling really confused. I don't know why I'm not living with you. Why am I living with someone else and visiting you in an office?" Instead the child might just walk over and start playing with a toy without saying hello. Most children behave their feelings and can't explain them in words.

Unless someone has told the parent in advance that it is fairly common for children to act this way during visits, many parents feel rejected if they don't get a hug or hello. They might feel disappointed and angry with the child, or feel upset with the foster parent, believing that the foster parent has set the child against them. That can set the visit off to a bad beginning.

Parents who understand their children's complicated feelings are more able to meet their needs. Parents can say to themselves, "I will go to my child and get on the floor and play even though my child hasn't said hello."

## Supporting the Parent
The visit coach's main role is to ask parents: "What does your child want from you?"

At first, parents often say, "My child wants to go home." That thinking can make planning a visit very difficult since that's the one need that the parent can't meet. Coaches help parents stand in the child's shoes and think, "What are the child's needs that I *can* meet?"

Parents might start with physical needs, like being hungry and needing food, or basic emotional needs, like, "My children need to know that I love them." The coach's role is to ask, "Well, what would make your child feel that you love them? What are the fun things that you did with your child before placement?"

## Making a Connection
Coaches can also help parents think about developmental needs. If a child is developing speech, the child needs to practice talking during visits. If the child is in elementary school, the child needs to tell the parent about friends and what they're doing in school.

The most important thing during visits is to get a back-and-forth going with your children, whether that's through singing a song, giving raspberries on the belly during the diaper change, smiling at each other, playing a game, or talking about school. With little kids, you might push cars around on the floor. Taking pictures, doing art, and even painting fingernails can be a time to listen to your child

talk about their lives and a way to make that special connection.

## Focus on Bonding
Visit Coaches can also help parents avoid one of the most common mistakes: using the visit time to talk with agency workers about their case. Parents do this because they feel that the top priority is to communicate with someone who can help with their case. But when parents use visits to talk with other adults instead of focusing on their children, caseworkers worry that the parent is not interested in the child.

When children are at home, many parents will give them a bottle or let them play while talking to another adult, and that's OK because they have many hours a day to build a connection with their child. When your child is in foster care, visits are the few short minutes you have each week to parent your child. You have to do all the connecting that you'd normally do in a week in one or two hours.

It's very sad for parents to think, "My child needs me to work hard to build our relationship while my child is in foster care." That's painful because no one wants to believe that a child's connection to her parent is fragile, or that the child may not be coming home very soon. But even a few weeks or months is a long time for a child to be apart from a parent. A child's attachment to the parent is like a flower—you have to water it regularly and give it sun.

Rise

## LEADER'S GUIDE:

**Eat, Play, Love** by Sylvia
Visits helped me become a good mother.

## TODAY WE'LL TALK ABOUT:
**How you can plan your visits**

### INTRODUCTION

It's important that you plan for visits ahead of time. You'll want to pack a snack, toys, books and baby gear, and plan activities that you and your child enjoy doing together. The main thing is that you want to have a lot of positive back-and-forth with your child. Games like peek-a-boo or pattycake might engage a baby. Songs or simple games like red-light/green-light and mother-may-I may keep young children engaged with you. Older children might enjoy puzzles or board games, and talking about friends and school.

Having a basic routine for every visit will also help your visits go smoothly. Routines are very important to children. Children feel safe and behave best when they know what to expect. After you say hello, you may want to start every visit with a snack, then play, then read a book together to provide a calming time before the visit ends. You may want to sing a favorite song together at the beginning or end of each visit, or say goodbye each week by talking about what you'll do together the next week.

Let's read Sylvia's story and think about planning positive visits.

### READ AND DISCUSS STORY

Let's take turns reading the story out loud. Who wants to start?

# Eat, Play, Love

*Visits helped me become a good mother.*

By Sylvia Perez

When my daughter, Lydia, was a year and a half, she was removed from home because my husband and I were using drugs. At our first visit, Hector and I were very anxious. I was scared that Little Mama would forget me, or would feel that I did not want her anymore.

Waiting in the hallway for our baby, we saw a Spanish man holding a little girl. The girl looked like my baby but she had bangs. Could that be her? My husband, Hector, said, "It is her" and he grabbed her from the guy's arms, saying, "Mama." She grabbed him back and put her little head on his shoulders.

When I saw my daughter's haircut, I was so upset. She did not look like my daughter. I confronted the worker and she told me that the foster parents could not see her eyes. I told her, "They should have put her hair up!"

"I'm sorry," the worker said. "It will grow back."

## Sad and Confused
During the visit, Little Mama would not let go of us and was quiet. Her eyes gave a blank stare, moving ever so slowly. We tried to play toys with her but she just wanted comfort. She wrapped her body around me and rested her head on my shoulder. Her father and I rubbed her back and told her that we loved her very much and would fight to get her home.

At the end of the visit, it was hard to say goodbye. Little Mama was crying so much. Her face was full of agony. She screamed, "Mommy! Daddy!" I can still remember her arms stretching out to us.

When I looked into her eyes, I felt despair and guilt. I cried and hugged and kissed Little Mama and told her we would see her again.

## A Mom, But Not a Good One
Before my daughter was removed, I had a very bad addiction for almost 20 years. At times, I barely slept or ate. I wandered the streets looking for my next hit. I had six children before Lydia and didn't raise any of them. Two of my sons ended up in foster care and were adopted

by their foster mom, Tamera, who I asked to take Lydia when she went into foster care.

When I got pregnant with Lydia, I was determined to raise her. I stayed clean for six months. But I relapsed, even though I loved my daughter with all my heart.

While I was using, I tried to take care of Lydia. I put her to sleep by laying her on my stomach and rubbing her back until she fell asleep. I held her and comforted her when she cried. Little Mama liked to be tickled on her tummy and she liked rolling a ball back and forth. When she was old enough, I would take her to the park and push her on the swing and help her climb the jungle gym.

The best thing I remember during that time was Lydia's first birthday. I planned and saved money. I made tuna salad, baked macaroni and cheese, *pernil*, chicken and green salad. We had a big cake with Baby Minnie. I had *capias* made for each guest. We taped the trees with streamers and I even had her father hang a piñata stuffed with candy. All of my friends came and Tamera and her husband came with my two sons. That was the best thing—spending the day with my two sons and my baby.

Lydia was laughing and playing. I don't think she understood what was going on, but she was very curious about her toys and ate a lot of cake. She even took her first steps that day.

Sometimes I was a good mom to Lydia but not always. Other times I would sell her milk and food stamps for money, and I would leave her in her crib while I got high. I hated when my high came down and I had to face that I'd messed up as a mother. That was the worst. I would lay on the floor with my daughter watching TV and I

would cry. My guilt was tremendous. I always prayed to God to forgive me.

### Getting Ready
After Lydia went into foster care, we had visits at an agency in the Bronx for two years. The visit room had a small red couch and some little chairs. There was a toy room but the lady in charge was rarely there. So basically, it looked like an office: no toys and very gloomy green paint on the walls.

A few days before each visit, I would pack a bag of toys and coloring books and reading books. I tried to be ready for any activity. Hector and I would go shopping to buy Little Mama a new outfit and things for her hair.

Little Mama would come wearing clothes that were too small, and her hair was never really done properly. So when Mama first came in to visits, I would hug her and then take her to the bathroom to change her clothes and do her hair.

### Eating and Playing
It made me feel better that I was still able to take care of my daughter. Even when I was using crack, I would get Lydia clothes from the church and wash them by hand so she would look like a clean little girl. With her hair done, she looked like my little angel again. I also loved to be in the bathroom with my daughter, away from everybody else. It was my time to comfort Lydia and let her know that I loved her.

Then Little Mama would usually eat a Happy Meal that Hector would bring for her, and for the rest of the visit, she and her father and I would play. Her favorite thing to do was color. She also liked us to bring kitchen things, like plates and spoons and forks. We would pretend we were cooking. Every visit, I brought a camera and took pictures to look at during my week.

When it was time to say goodbye, I tried not to cry because I did not want Lydia to see me hysterical. I would tell her, "I love you and I'll see you next week." Hector would ask, "What do you want us to bring to the next visit?" As she got older, she could tell us if she wanted any candy or a toy. Then we would say goodbye with a hug and a kiss.

### Smothering Her With Love
When the judge gave my family unsupervised visits, it was such a weight off to leave the agency. I was able to really hold my daughter and smother her with all of my love. She would call out, "Mommy!" and give me hugs and kisses. The more time I had with Lydia, the more connection I felt to her.

We would pick her up at 10 a.m. and bring her back by 4 p.m. We always made sure we were there early to pick her up and on time to drop her off. We would take her out to lunch, to the pool, the park and the playground, and to see all of our friends.

I loved taking her to the swimming pool. I bought her a little sky blue one-piece bathing suit. I would take her in the baby pool and watch her try to swim in the water. Now that I was sober, I was able to laugh and play in the water with her without any shame. My daughter's father would meet us at the pool and we would go for lunch. These were moments that I did not want to let go of.

### A Good Mother
Being out with Lydia sober was so much better. My thoughts were clear and I was able to take time to enjoy her laughter and her ideas.

I had never been sure that I could be a good mom. I was not raised by my mother; I was raised by the system. Not having a mom or dad for guidance when I became a mother was very hard. During moments when I felt I needed advice, I felt empty. Feeling empty and alone had fed my addiction.

In parenting classes I learned that I could become a real parent to my daughter and have family activities with her and my husband. I learned about unconditional love and how to show Little Mama my love.

During visits, I was able to do motherly things with Lydia, like saying "I love you" and playing with her. I learned that I could be a good mother. I also found out that I am a responsible person. I was proud that I was able to plan outings with Lydia and make sure that I had packed what she needed, like milk, juice, diapers and a change of clothes.

### The Little Things
The best parts of our visits were the little things: being able to hear her say "Mommy" and feeling her hand in mine. Away from the agency, I felt safe with her, like no one could take Lydia from me.

Simple things felt good to me, like eating at a Chinese restaurant together, or asking Lydia about her brothers and Tamera and how things were in her foster home. The best was taking Lydia to church with me. I was able to put her in a nice dress and shoes and finally introduce her to people there. That was something I had wanted for a long time.

## NOW LET'S TALK ABOUT THE STORY:

• What did Sylvia think her daughter needed from her during visits?

• What did Sylvia and Hector do to plan positive visits?

• What routine did Sylvia, Hector and Lydia follow during visits?

• How do you think their activities helped them bond?

• How did Sylvia end visits and why did she say goodbye that way?

## PERSONAL REFLECTION TIME

Let's look at the worksheet called "My Reflections." Take 5 or 10 minutes to write down your answers on the worksheet and then we'll share. (*Wait until most people are finished.*)

• Who wants to share their responses?

## ENDING THE GROUP

Now turn to the "Visit Journal" worksheet. Take a few minutes to write down your goal for this week's visit. You can answer the "reflection" questions and fill in the checklist after your visit. Please do that at home.

Next week, we'll start by talking about your visits. I look forward to hearing from everyone about how you tried to reach your goals!

## NEXT WEEK

Let's talk about how your visits went this week:
• Who tried to meet their goal? How did it go?
• Will someone share a moment they are proud of?
• Will someone talk about something they'd handle differently next time?
Thank you for sharing.

## My Reflections: Eat, Play, Love by Sylvia Perez

1. How do you plan visits with your children? What planning could you do?

2. What activities do you and your children enjoy doing together? What might you enjoy?

3. What is a basic routine that you could get into?

4. How do you—or how could you—say goodbye in a positive way?

## My Visit Journal – Eat, Play, Love

**GOAL:** Look over your children's needs that you identified last week. What activities can you do this week to help you connect with your children? What's a routine that could make visits more positive?

**REFLECTION:** What planning did you do before your visit? What impact did your planning have on the visits?

Did you follow the routine and do the activities you planned? How did it go?

What's something you did during your visit that you feel proud of?

OVER ⟶

## My Visit Journal Checklist: Eat, Play, Love by Sylvia Perez

Please use the checklist below to keep track of the steps you are taking to improve your visits. Use the "comments" section to make notes about your experiences.

| Did I... | Comments |
|---|---|
| ☐ Attend my visit | |
| ☐ Arrive on time | |
| ☐ Plan activities | |
| ☐ Bring toys | |
| ☐ Bring a snack | |
| ☐ Greet my child's foster parent | |
| ☐ Keep anger/frustration out of my visit | |
| ☐ Focus only on my child | |

| Did I respond to my child's needs... | |
|---|---|
| ☐ for me to be trustworthy | |
| ☐ to follow a routine | |
| ☐ to have fun together | |
| ☐ to eat together | |
| ☐ to feel safe with the foster parent | |
| ☐ to talk about experiences in foster care | |
| ☐ to say goodbye in a positive way | |

# Bonding with Baby

*How to strengthen your connection to your infant.*

By Sabra Jackson

*My son was taken from me straight from the hospital because he was born positive tox. At first, I saw him weekly with my older daughter, who was 7. I would whisper in his ear, "Mommy loves you, and you're coming home soon." He was so little I had to give him something that would help him connect to me.*

*But I felt very disconnected. So three times I asked for "bonding visits"—which are twice a week—until I finally got a court order to make them happen. Then I would bring special treats for him and we'd have our Mommy Time.*

*I think it helped, because when he came home after 11 months, I would pick him up and gently whisper, "You're home now. Mommy loves you." He would light up.*

*Still, it's very hard to bond when your baby is in foster care. To find out how parents can connect with their babies, I talked with Mary Dozier, a professor at the University of Delaware who helps birth parents and foster parents bond with their babies.*

**Q: What kind of care do babies need to develop strong bonds with their parents?**
**A:** It's very important to have nurturing, stable care from someone who is very highly committed to the child. The baby needs to know that somebody is going to be there for him and respond to his needs.

Babies are biologically wired to have a caregiver who's going to be there no matter what. There's a range of situations that babies can adapt to—like being in childcare, or having a babysitter—but it really challenges babies beyond what they can deal with to have caregivers who are not committed to them or to change from one caregiver to another.

**Q: How does it affect babies to move from one caregiver to another?**
**A:** When babies move from one home to another, it's hard for the baby to trust the new caregiver. We've been studying how moves affect babies' bodies and behavior.

We see that babies who've been moved around tend to push away their caregivers or cannot be soothed when they're upset. Because they push away help, these babies look like they don't need care, and their caregivers respond by giving them less attention.

If you are a birth parent who is reuniting with your baby, you can be hurt so badly if your baby acts like he doesn't need you or pushes you away. We do a lot of work with birth parents to help them see it's not personal. The child had to adapt in this way just to deal with multiple separations. And the good news is that babies' behavior can change if the parents know how to respond.

**Q: How can parents and babies bond?**
**A:** To help parents bond with their babies, we do a 10-session intervention with the mom and her baby. We try to get them to learn a few things:

First, parents need to very gently provide nurturance and affection even though the child doesn't seem to want it. It's hard for the parent not to start to assume, "He doesn't need me," or, "I haven't been with him and he doesn't care about me anymore." I know that from personal experience. I was divorced when my kids were 2 and 4, and when my 2-year-old started visiting his dad, he'd come back so mad because I hadn't been with him. He'd lash out and even hit me.

My normal instinct would be to say, "Don't do that. You can't hit me." But I was studying kids' development, so one day I said, "I think you're mad because I wasn't with you last night." He said, "That's why I'm mad!" and we had a real connection. He needed me to recognize how he was feeling.

The second important task is for parents to learn how to nurture their babies. Lots of us as parents are not naturally nurturing, so you have to override your instincts. Say a child falls and hits his head, and cries. We don't want parents to just say, "That didn't hurt!" Instead, the parents can gently pat the baby's back and say, "Oh, honey, that hurts, doesn't it?" We videotape the moms with their babies and then review the videos with them. We help

them see what their automatic response is and begin to make different kinds of responses.

The third thing we help parents learn is to follow the baby's lead and create a warm, delighted relationship with their child. Suppose that a mom isn't showing a lot of excitement in taking care of her baby. We use the videotapes to help the mom see when she and her baby are connecting and when they're not. So you might see the child throwing a toy on the floor and Mom not giving it back or smiling. Well, the mom might not realize it's a game, and that the baby's showing her that he's so excited and engaged.

If every once in a while you see Mom smiling at her child, then we really focus on his response and say, "He just lights up when you do that." Often, moms are able to say, "I didn't do it there, and look how he got sad."

**Q: What are some signs that parents and their babies might need extra help reconnecting?**
**A:** One sign is that someone says, "Oh, this child is just doing great. He's not upset by the move at all. He never cries, he doesn't ask anything of me." You don't want a child that doesn't show distress at all. You want him to trust in his caregiver to help him with his distress. If the child has pulled into himself and does not depend on anybody, I would worry about that.

I always tell parents, "Babies shouldn't be easy." It's not that they shouldn't be pleasant and happy, but a baby who's willing to sit in a carrier for hours is not doing well. The baby should be crawling on adults. We really want babies that ask a lot of their worlds.

## LEADER'S GUIDE:

**'Your Actions Are Setting You Back'** by Jeanette Vega
Losing my temper in visits hurt my case.

---

## TODAY WE'LL TALK ABOUT:
### Handling anger and frustration during visits

---

### INTRODUCTION

Parents may have many reasons to feel angry or upset during visits. Just arriving at the agency, or seeing your child with her foster parent, may remind you of all the frustration and sadness of being apart from your child. Little things that the foster parent does differently might upset you. Your child's behavior during visits may be different from how she behaved at home, leaving you feeling worried or frustrated. It's important to recognize that visiting might be stressful and upsetting. Even so, no matter how you feel during visits, it's essential that you keep your cool.

If you yell at or hit your children, child's foster parents, or agency staff, it will set you back in reunifying with your child, no matter how justifiable your anger may seem. Exploding during a visit shows agency staff that you cannot maintain self-control or stay focused on your child's needs. You will likely be referred to take an anger management class or have your visits reduced, jeopardizing reunification. Let's read Jeanette's story and think about how to keep cool despite the stresses of visiting.

---

### READ AND DISCUSS STORY

Let's take turns reading the story out loud. Who wants to start?

---

# 'Your Actions Are Setting You Back'

*Losing my temper in visits hurt my case.*

By Jeanette Vega

In 1999, my 2-year-old son Remi was removed because I hit him and my family called child welfare on me. I was only 17 years old when Remi was born and I didn't know how to handle my son. Remi was an all-over-the-place, running around, never-sitting-still type of kid. It was partially my fault. I spoiled him rotten. I thought that's what I was supposed to do—spoil him and love him to death.

I didn't know that Remi would get so out of control and never want to listen to me. By age 2, he was defiant and strong-minded. He wanted his way. Yes, he was 2, but I think it was more than that—Remi was recently diagnosed with ADHD. Back then, I did not know how to get him to listen. Besides, in my family, we were raised that if you talk back or get out line, you get your ass kicked.

One night while I was in the shower, Remi climbed out of his crib and went out to the sidewalk all by himself. When I saw that he was missing from our apartment and found him playing outside, I was shocked and scared and I hit

him. I immediately regretted it but the damage was done. When my mom and aunt saw the bruises the next day, they thought the best thing to do was call child welfare. Remi was removed and I was arrested.

### 'I'm Sorry, My Baby'

Our first few visits were rough. I felt as if I'd lost Remi's love and that his foster parents had made me out to be a monster. Remi seemed scared of me. He would hesitate to hug me, or hug me and then go back to the foster mother as if I would hurt him. It killed me. At those moments, I would break down and cry, apologizing to Remi: "I'm sorry, my baby. Mommy won't ever hurt you again. Life will be better for us."

Most times, Remi was quiet on my lap during visits, just hugging me while I whispered to him our song, "You Are My Sunshine." Remi was not playful or happy. Before going into care, he loved playing with his Ninja Turtle toys. I brought a new one to each visit, but he had no reaction of excitement. Remi's sadness also made it seem like everything I said he had done at home was a lie. He seemed to be a quiet, easy kid.

After a few weeks, Remi began to flip out at the end of visits. It felt good that my baby once again wanted only Mom. But it was awful to see him crying even harder than me. How do you explain to a 2 year old, "No, you have to leave with these people. I'll see you next week." I would cry on my way home, thinking, "How am I going to do this? I have to be strong for him."

Our first three months, the visits were supervised. They felt like jail. The foster mother, a nasty woman in her 30s, usually sat in the visit room along with her three teenagers and the worker. Being watched and told how to talk or play with my own child drove me crazy. I felt so uncomfortable that I just wanted the visits to end. I wanted to see Remi but it felt like there was no space for Remi and me to bond.

### Bottled Up
That first year that Remi was in care, I had such a hard time. I was angry that my family had called in the case and that they did not step up to care for Remi. (My aunt took him for one week— then she realized that she couldn't handle him, either, and she turned him in to the system.) For a long time, I didn't speak to any family members.

Then I lost my grandmother and my big brother, who was my everything. I felt like I was losing everything and everyone slowly. I was devastated. There was nothing I wanted to do. I felt weak and hopeless. To deal with feeling that others saw me as a child abuser, I put up a front of "I am strong, nothing bothers me." It felt like my only way to get through it all. I feared that if I let myself feel what I was feeling, I might not have the strength to get Remi back.

The agency recommended that I seek counseling, but that didn't work. I was not open to speaking to someone I didn't know. The only person I let in on my heartbreak was my fiancé. He didn't care how I pushed him away and shut down. He took care of me and guided me to be strong. He truly saved Remi, because I almost could not breathe.

### My Pain, My Anger, My Hurt
One day, after he had been in care for a year, Remi came in with stitches on his chin. The foster mother said that he had run into a computer table. At that moment, I froze up and freaked out, thinking, "They take him from me for hitting him yet they bring him to me with stitches?" I believed that her teenagers had been playing too rough and the mother had covered it up.

I felt like I had taken all I could take. Remi was only three and helpless to protect himself. I grabbed the foster mother's neck and kept squeezing until the workers took me off. That foster mother felt all my pain, my anger, my hurt.

When I let go, I saw that Remi was scared, and for frightening him I was truly sorry. I told Remi, "I love you and I am not mad at you. They hurt you and that is a no-no."

I told the worker, "She ain't taking my baby nowhere."

I told the foster mom, "Trust me, I will sleep in front of your house to make sure you don't do anything to him."

The foster mother left, saying, "I am not putting up with this."

After that incident, Remi was placed with another foster mom. My first impression was that

Gladys seemed decent enough. Her kids were grown and she had time to get to know Remi. I was relieved.

But my unsupervised visits were suspended and the workers gave me anger management classes. I thought, "As if I had no reason to be angry!" I felt that the child welfare system was what made me angry and I felt justified in attacking Remi's foster mom. I was sure that she had hurt my baby and that no one cared.

### Sent Back

A few months later, I was sitting on the floor with Remi, playing "Itsy Bitsy Spider." The worker came in and said, "You should be doing something educational, or reading to him."

"Really, you have the nerve to come in this tiny room with baby chairs and a table and tell me to read to him. He is 3 years old! He wants to go outside and run and jump!" I said. I felt they had us like prisoners in that room.

She screamed at me, saying, "You can go. I will cancel your visit if you want to have an attitude."

"You do what you want and let me bond with my son how we want. Who the hell are you to tell me what he likes and dislikes?" I said. I cursed at her and Remi started crying.

I had just finished one anger management class, but I was sent back to take another.

### More Time Together

Luckily, Remi's foster mom saw our pain. I asked Gladys if I could attend Remi's doctor visits, school meetings and therapy, and share his first day of camp. I also asked if I could walk home with her and Remi after school, just to see how his day went. Gladys thought that he and I be-

longed together and needed more time together, so she made it happen!

After school, I would often walk home with them, help Remi with homework, eat dinner with their family, and even put him to bed. She'd always tell Remi, "You are going home with Mommy soon and you will always be welcome here. You will have two homes when you go back to live with Mom for good."

Gladys loved Remi and made him part of her family. At Christmas, she invited me to come over. Everyone knew him and bought him gifts, and he got hugs and kisses just like the grand-kids. It was a great sight to see but heartbreak-ing at the same time. I felt like such an outsider. Part of me wanted to snatch him up and say, "They are not your family, I am!" But it was not his fault he ended up there, and I was happy see him in such a loving, caring family.

### 'Are You Serious?'

When Remi had been with Gladys for a year (and in foster care for two years), I was almost done with all my services and was pushing for weekend visits.

Then one day, my latest worker (I had five in all) told me that my fiancé would have to do all the services I'd done before Remi could come home. That was going to take an entire year! I felt so trapped and bad and overwhelmed that I don't even know how to express it.

Soon after, I took Remi on an unsupervised visit to Chuck E. Cheese. He loved it, and I loved it. We had so much fun together. Then I realized that we were 30 minutes late to get back to the agency. I rushed Remi out of there and we took a cab back.

The worker was outside with Gladys and the police. "Oh my God," I thought. "Really? Is it that serious?" The worker said it was procedure because they thought I had taken him and run. She also said that we'd start supervised visits again. I was so frustrated that I cursed her out.

### 'Can I Speak to You?'

This time, my worker pulled me aside. "Can I speak to you?" she said. "I am not here to argue with you. I just want you to understand that your actions are setting you back."

"But I'm sick of people trying to tell me how to live my life and how to act with my son. It's insane," I said.

"It might seem that way now, but in the long run, you can be with your son. Try not to let things upset you, or try not show anger when something occurs that frustrates you."

"Everyone thinks that because I'm young they can talk to me like they want," I told her. "If they want respect, they need to show respect."

"I will try to talk to you in an appropriate manner," she told me.

"I will do my best to keep my cool for Remi's sake," I said.

Up until then, I hadn't really understood how my actions were seen. But it did sink in that I was making things worse for Remi. I decided to try to ignore what workers said to me, even if I didn't agree or didn't like the way they talked to me. I didn't want to be the cause of my son staying in care longer.

### The Worst in Me

In the end, it took three years for my son to come home. Looking back, I wish I did things differently. I am sorry that I hurt the foster mother and that I hurt my son. At that time in my life, I really did not know that telling the workers how I felt would set me back for months. Now I realize that the workers saw me as someone who would try to fix any situation with hitting, and my actions did hurt my case.

But I also wish that the caseworkers could've seen me as a naïve young mother who was raised in a neighborhood where, if you get tough, you get put in your place. I felt that the workers were testing me and wanted me to fail, and that I needed to show them how tough I could be.

The workers had so much power over me, and I was in such an extreme emotional battle within myself. I really needed them to stay calm and explain things to me in a reasonable way. Instead, the workers were quick to judge me and took the worst out of me.

### Actions Have Consequences

Ten years later, I'm no longer a naïve teenage mother. I've learned that the way that you portray yourself in life is how you get treated, and that little mistakes can make a world of difference. As an advocate, I tell other parents to stay cool and collected. They need to show the worker that they can control themselves.

I've also learned how to be much more patient and understanding. Remi is a teenager now, and I have two little boys. I try to show my children that our actions have consequences, and that no matter how right you may feel that you are, you have the choice to deal with things in a positive way. I have grown a lot. I want my children to know that mom gets mad but always keeps her cool.

## NOW LET'S TALK ABOUT THE STORY:

• What different emotions was Jeanette dealing with during visits?

• How did Jeanette's feelings make it difficult to stay calm and focused on her son?

• How did the visit conditions contribute to her stress?

• How might it have affected Jeanette's son to see her getting so angry?

• How else could Jeanette have handled those difficult moments?

## PERSONAL REFLECTION TIME

Let's look at the worksheet called "My Reflections." Take 5 or 10 minutes to write down your answers on the worksheet and then we'll share. (*Wait until most people are finished.*)

• Who wants to share their responses?

## ENDING THE GROUP

Now turn to the "Visit Journal" worksheet. Take a few minutes to write down your goal for this week's visit. You can answer the "reflection" questions and fill in the checklist after your visit. Please do that at home.

Next week, we'll start by talking about your visits. I look forward to hearing from everyone about how you tried to reach your goals!

## NEXT WEEK

Let's talk about how your visits went this week:
• Who tried to meet their goal? How did it go?
• Will someone share a moment they are proud of?
• Will someone talk about something they'd handle differently next time?

Thank you for sharing.

Rise

## My Reflections: 'Your Actions Are Setting You Back' by Jeanette Vega

1. What difficult feelings are you dealing with during visits?

2. What makes it hard to keep anger or frustration from disrupting your visits?

3. How might your anger or painful feelings be affecting your child or your case?

4. What might help you feel or act more positive during visits?

## My Visit Journal – 'Your Actions Are Setting You Back'

**GOALS:** Write down one or two steps you could take to arrive at visits feeling or acting more positive or to keep anger out of your visit.

What activities and routines will help you feel positive and connected with your child?

**REFLECTION:** Did you do what you planned in order to feel more positive during visits? How did it go?

What's something you did to keep anger out of your visit that you feel proud of?

OVER ⟶

Rise

## My Visit Journal Checklist: 'Your Actions Are Setting You Back' by Jeanette Vega

Please use the checklist below to keep track of the steps you are taking to improve your visits. Use the "comments" section to make notes about your experiences.

| Did I... | Comments |
|---|---|
| ☐ Attend my visit | |
| ☐ Arrive on time | |
| ☐ Plan activities | |
| ☐ Bring toys | |
| ☐ Bring a snack | |
| ☐ Greet my child's foster parent | |
| ☐ Keep anger/frustration out of my visit | |
| ☐ Focus only on my child | |

Did I respond to my child's needs...

| | |
|---|---|
| ☐ for me to be trustworthy | |
| ☐ to follow a routine | |
| ☐ to have fun together | |
| ☐ to eat together | |
| ☐ to feel safe with the foster parent | |
| ☐ to talk about experiences in foster care | |
| ☐ to say goodbye in a positive way | |

**LEADER'S GUIDE:**

**Waiting My Turn** by Latonya Baskerville
I had to let my grandmother be the parent until
my kids returned home.

---

**TODAY WE'LL TALK ABOUT:**
Communicating with your child's foster parents

---

**INTRODUCTION**

It's important that parents find positive ways to communicate with their child's foster parent. When parents and foster parents exchange information about the child and work together to make visits positive, kids get better care while in foster care and go home more quickly.

Most of all, when parents and foster parents communicate, kids feel less worried. Many kids in foster care are worried about loyalty—if they like the foster parent, does that mean they can't like their parent anymore? Sometimes children will misbehave in the foster home just to reassure their parents of their love. Children behave better and feel better if they see that their parent and foster parent are not in conflict and that everyone can get along.

You may feel jealous and sad when you see your child and her foster parent together. Even so, simple things—like saying hello and goodbye to your child's foster parent at visits, asking the foster parent about the child's week, and staying positive about the foster parent in front of your child during visits—can improve your visits and make life in foster care much less stressful for your child.

Let's read Latonya's story.

---

**READ AND DISCUSS STORY**

Let's take turns reading the story out loud. Who wants to start?

# Waiting My Turn

*I had to let my grandmother be the parent until my kids returned home.*

By Latonya Baskerville

My children were placed in kinship care with my grandmother in August 1998. At first I thought this was a wonderful arrangement. My grandmother raised my brother and me. We were removed from my mother's care when I was 8 and he was 6 because of my mother's mental health.

Even though my grandmother had an old-fashioned parenting style, I knew she would be better for my children than a stranger. Also, I had a lot of perks while my children were with my grandmother. Sometimes I would spend the night with them, or my grandmother would give me money and take me shopping. I would take the children to neighborhood functions and parks. It was like my kids and I were living with my grandmother.

But I had so much freedom that I did not comply with drug treatment or the foster care agency.

## My Kids, My Way

After a few months, the kinship arrangement began to frustrate me. I didn't like some of the ways my grandmother had treated me as a child.

She was now treating my kids the same way. My grandmother belittles to encourage, meaning that if a child doesn't clean, you call her nasty; if a person is overweight, you call her a pig; if she doesn't have a job, you call her lazy or a bum; if a teen has sex, you call her a whore.

My grandmother also doesn't believe in negotiating with a child or adjusting her expectations for any reason. My children loved summer nights when it was cool and light outside and other kids were still out playing on our block. If there's no school in the morning, I think it's OK to stay up later. No, not OK with grandma. Bedtime was 8 pm year-round.

Through the foster care agency, I took parenting skills training and I wanted to stop using my grandmother's parenting model. I believed that a parent can make the rules clear but also listen to children and negotiate. I also believed that children can be spoken to with respect, and that children have the right to respectfully speak their minds and be acknowledged as decision-makers in a household.

### 'I Got Custody, Not You'

One day, I decided to try a parenting technique I had learned. That afternoon I was outside with my kids and all the other families on the block. My 16-month-old got in a tugging match over a bike with another child. Instead of yelling, I said to my baby, "That bike is not yours. You must give it back."

Then my grandmother yelled out in front of everyone, "You don't say nothing to him. I got custody of him, not you." I was devastated. I could not believe that she would say that to me in front of all these people.

Still, I knew I couldn't just blame my grandmother for the situation. I was the one not taking care of my responsibilities. My grandmother probably lashed out because she was tired and fed up. She had taken care of my siblings and me because our mother was mentally ill, but I was not.

That night, I was angry as heck at myself. I sat up crying at what my substance abuse did to my family and me. I thought, "Here I am, messed up and blaming my 65-year-old grandmother for my mistakes and bad decisions."

### My Breaking Point

That day was her breaking point, and it was mine, too. The shame and guilt I felt were hard to bear. I was not high anymore so I felt every feeling, and the reality that my children were not mine to parent was too painful to ignore.

After my shock subsided I realized I could no longer play around with the system. Soon I began to take responsibility for my actions and my situation. I began complying with my service plan.

I still thought that, after I got my kids home, I would go back to using drugs. But as I got encouragement and support from the staff, I began to focus on my children and becoming a better parent to them. I began my journey in recovery.

### Focusing on the Future

During the 18 months that my children were in my grandmother's care, I forced myself to look past her negative comments. Even though she did some things that did not please me, I forgave her because her love for my children and me was obvious.

I didn't talk with her about how I felt. I figured it would be a wasted discussion. Instead, I reminded myself, "She is a loving and caring grandmother who is extending herself because of my mistakes and bad decisions. At 65, she's getting up all night with a newborn while taking care of two older children." I knew that raising my children was not easy for her, and I felt that it was more important to focus on the future than on the past.

### My Children Were Confused

Still, it was not easy while my children were still living in her home. I saw that my children were so confused when my grandmother and I were both in the room. They didn't understand who had the authority.

My children's confusion was evident one day when I told my 10-year-old son that he was not getting a videogame because of his behavior in school. My grandmother bought the game for him anyway. When I saw him with it, I asked him, "Didn't I say you couldn't have the game?"

"Grandma bought it," he said. "I told her you said no because of my school behavior."

I was upset, but I let her maintain the authority role until my kids were returned to my care.

### 'They're Yours'

When I regained custody, I thought the transition would be hard for my grandmother and me but it was not. At our final discharge meeting, I felt good because I saw that my grandmother was anxious to give me back my parental role. She said, "Here they are. They're yours." We laughed and went out together to a restaurant to celebrate.

My grandmother told me then, "I knew that you would get your children back." She added, "It was so amazing how the baby up and left when I told him he was going home. He felt good going home. That is truly a blessing from God."

It helped that I lived with my children in my grandmother's home and she moved out, so my children stayed in the same schools and slept in the same rooms. The only change was their parental figure.

### Everyone Had to Adjust

Still, it took all of us a while to adjust to the changes. I was so happy to have my children back but I was also sober and very afraid. Things were a little crazy for a while. My children were angry that they had been in foster care and they didn't trust me. They threw every name at me and I had to find a way to stay calm.

I told my children. "I really want to stop yelling and spanking. I've learned a new way to parent and this is the way we are going to live." We all agreed. We created new house rules, we rotated chores every month, and had family meetings regularly.

I also put up neon behavior charts. If my kids followed house rules, I rewarded them every pay period. If not, I rewarded myself. My children soon realized that I wouldn't yell and scream anymore when they didn't do their chores or when they misbehaved at school or at home. I would just go shopping.

### Close and Connected

My grandmother had to adjust to the new rules, too. She kept coming in and trying to re-organize my home. I respectfully told her again and again, "Thank you so much for helping me when I was down but I am well now and my children must abide by my rules." We had many struggles but we got through them.

Now, almost 10 years later, we are all much older and doing fine. My children and I continue to have a close relationship with my grandmother. My 20-year-old son lives in one of my grandmother's buildings, my daughter just moved back into my house after being with my grandmother for two years, and my baby is home. We all visit my grandmother as much as possible. She is over 75 now. In the summer, we sit outside with her and barbecue.

I am glad I was able to respect my grandmother's parenting style and that she respects mine. Our relationship was not destroyed by the conflicts we faced while my children were in her care.

## NOW LET'S TALK ABOUT THE STORY:

• What made Latonya's children feel confused about who had the authority in their family?

• How do you think it might have affected Latonya's children to feel caught between their mother and their grandmother?

• What was positive about how Latonya handled the situation?

• How might Latonya have tried to talk with her grandmother in order to work together so her children felt safer and less confused?

• How could Latonya have helped her children understand the situation?

## PERSONAL REFLECTION TIME

Let's look at the worksheet called "My Reflections." Take 5 or 10 minutes to write down your answers on the worksheet and then we'll share. (*Wait until most people are finished.*)

• Who wants to share their responses?

## ENDING THE GROUP

Now turn to the "Visit Journal" worksheet. Take a few minutes to write down your goal for this week's visit. You can answer the "reflection" questions and fill in the checklist" after your visit. Please do that at home.

Next week, we'll start by talking about your visits. I look forward to hearing from everyone about how you tried to reach your goals!

## NEXT WEEK

Let's talk about how your visits went this week:
• Who tried to meet their goal? How did it go?
• Will someone share a moment they are proud of?
• Will someone talk about something they'd handle differently next time?

Thank you for sharing.

## My Reflections: Waiting My Turn by Latonya Baskerville

1. What's positive about your relationship with your child's foster parents? What's negative?

2. How do you think your children may be affected by your relationship with their foster parents?

3. What are some small things that you could do to make a more positive connection with your child's foster parent at the visit?

## My Visit Journal – Waiting My Turn

**GOAL:** What's one thing you can do to make a more positive connection with your child's foster parent during the visit?

**REFLECTION:** Did you do what you planned to make a more positive connection with your child's foster parent during the visit? How did it go?

What's something that you did to keep anger out your visit that you feel proud of?

What's something you did to connect with your child that you feel proud of?

OVER ⟶

## My Visit Journal Checklist: Waiting My Turn by Latonya Baskerville

Please use the checklist below to keep track of the steps you are taking to improve your visits. Use the "comments" section to make notes about your experiences.

| Did I... | Comments |
|---|---|
| ☐ Attend my visit | |
| ☐ Arrive on time | |
| ☐ Plan activities | |
| ☐ Bring toys | |
| ☐ Bring a snack | |
| ☐ Greet my child's foster parent | |
| ☐ Keep anger/frustration out of my visit | |
| ☐ Focus only on my child | |
| Did I respond to my child's needs... | |
| ☐ for me to be trustworthy | |
| ☐ to follow a routine | |
| ☐ to have fun together | |
| ☐ to eat together | |
| ☐ to feel safe with the foster parent | |
| ☐ to talk about experiences in foster care | |
| ☐ to say goodbye in a positive way | |

# Out on the Town

*Visit Hosts help families reconnect outside of agency visit rooms.*

By Damaris Figueroa

Last year, I signed up to be trained as a Visit Host—someone who can supervise family visits outside of foster care agency visit rooms. Visit Hosting allows families the opportunity to do all the things that families usually do together, like eat out and go to activities in their communities.

In the training at Children's Services, a New York City child welfare agency, I learned about the responsibility that comes with hosting visits. Visit Hosts must ensure that the child is safe during visits and write a report about each visit. Before I was matched with a family, I was afraid that I wouldn't be effective or helpful, and I wasn't sure what the visits would be like.

### Exciting Activities

I began hosting visits for a couple and their beautiful 2-year-old daughter. We started out with three-hour visits every Tuesday and Thursday. We did activities like eating out at an Italian restaurant and bagel places, visiting the Museum of Natural History and going to the movies and Central Park. The mom was very creative and she would bring party hats and little horns that we would blow.

It was exciting for the parents and their daughter to visit outside the agency visit room. It was exciting for me, too, because I did things I'd never done before. I saw the Christmas tree at Rockefeller Center for the first time, tried scallops at a fancy Chinese restaurant, and went to a parade in Little Italy. Whatever we did, it was always fun and interesting. It seemed easier for the family to become closer while seeing new things and going different places.

By the third visit, my worries had disappeared. I was getting along great with the family and I even felt comfortable writing the reports.

### Comfortable and Affectionate

As I got more comfortable, the little girl got comfortable with her family and with me. At first, she would not talk to or even look at me. When we were at a restaurant, she was distracted and just wanted to run around.

As time went on, the little girl grew increasingly more affectionate with her parents. She began to talk more and sit still, close to her parents, and actually eat her food if we ate out. Soon everything came to be about Mommy and Daddy. If she was sleepy, the little girl would call for Daddy. He would

*continued on next page*

continued from previous page
carry her and she would fall asleep on his shoulders or in his arms.

The little girl looked forward to our adventures. If I got to her foster home first on visit days, she would be eagerly waiting for the doorbell to ring again and her parents to arrive.

As the family grew closer, I grew close to them, too. They felt like part of my family. I even brought my 9-year-old son on a couple of visits and to the agency's Christmas party. He got along beautifully with the little girl.

### Sad to Say Goodbye

For a while, the visits were going very well. Other parents at the foster care agency began hearing about the family's great experiences and would beg me to be their Visit Host. The judge even granted the family an additional two hours on Tuesdays and Thursdays. I felt so good.

But after 7 months, I had to stop hosting the family's visits. Money ran out to pay me for my work, and the agency did not feel that the family was heading toward reunification after all. The judge ruled that the mom could have unsupervised visits but, without a Visit Host, the dad had to visit at the agency visit room again.

For our last visit together, we went to the movies and the visit went well, as usual, but it was sad. The mom was angry about the visit hosting ending, and I was sad that I wouldn't see the little girl anymore. She has been separated from her family for so long and now is being separated from me, another person who came into her life.

I hope that I will get the chance to be a Visit Host to another family. It also makes me sad and angry at the same time when I think of how many other families have children in foster care and never get to experience positive times with their children outside of agency visit rooms.

# LEADER'S GUIDE:

**Breaking a Painful Pattern** by Milagros Sanchez
My children won't grow up silenced and afraid.

---

## TODAY WE'LL TALK ABOUT:
Talking to your kids about foster care

---

### INTRODUCTION

Children in foster care usually blame themselves for being in foster care. Developmentally, children believe the world revolves around them. When bad things happen, children believe they're at fault. On top of all of the stresses of living in foster care, children are burdened by guilt and shame.

Your children need you to tell them that it is not their fault that they are in foster care. No matter what happened, fair or unfair, that led your children to be placed in foster care, it's important that your children understand that they didn't cause the problem and that they can't solve it, either. Sometimes children act up while in foster care, hoping to be sent home. Your children need to know that *your* actions, not theirs, will determine whether they return home.

Your children also need you to listen to them talk about their experiences in foster care. Hearing what they are going through without you can feel confusing and sad. You may feel very powerless or even jealous. But listening to your child will help your child heal. Let's read Milagros' story about opening up communication in her family.

---

### READ AND DISCUSS STORY

Let's take turns reading the story out loud. Who wants to start?

# Breaking a Painful Pattern

*My children won't grow up silenced and afraid.*

By Milagros Sanchez

On Aug. 4, 1997, I got my sons back after they'd been in foster care and I'd been out on the streets for many years. I felt that God had given me a second chance in life to be the best mom I could be.

### Determined to Be Different

I was determined to be different toward my sons than my mother had been toward me. My mother and I had a bad relationship when I was a child. She resorted to violence whenever she was upset with me, and she didn't believe me when I came to her and told her I was being sexually abused. When I was a teenager, she put me in a group home, where I was sexually abused again.

As a child, I was always told, "What happens at home stays at home." Since what happened to me was taboo to talk about, I buried my pain inside but acted it out by being very rebellious, using alcohol at a very young age and, eventually, taking drugs. But in rehab, I found that it was all right to express myself. Slowly but surely I started talking about my feelings, even to my

mother.

My mom was very closed at the beginning. There was a lot of shouting and screaming, but one day she said to me, "I know I have not been the best person or mother to you. But I'm sorry for not being there for you. I'll try my best to be there for your boys. I love you." I know that was very difficult for her because my mom never told any one of us that she loved us.

### A Family Pattern

Slowly, our relationship improved. We talked more about the mistakes she made raising me, and we made it a point to forgive one another. I found out by talking to her about her childhood that my mom never was taught how to converse with her children, but only to get physical when things went wrong.

When I learned about my mother's upbringing, I realized that my family had a pattern of not speaking about feelings and of physically abusing children. I told myself, "I will make it my business to change that pattern when I get my life together."

## Family Conferences

In the months before they returned home I built a bond with my boys. We spent every other weekend together and I always had something planned for us to do as a family. We went out to the movies, the beach, or the pool, and to museums and the library. Sometimes we would just stay home and play family games. I would also make them their favorite foods.

Every Friday we had a family conference. That was a chance for my sons to let out their feelings about what they went through. They were allowed to ask me any questions they wanted about my addiction and the time when I was not with them. Answering their questions, I would get very emotional, but it helped us get closer. It was a step toward breaking the silence and anger that had dominated my family's relationships for too long.

My son JonPaul asked me why I left him with grandma for such a long time. He said, "Didn't you love us? Was it something we did?" It was very hard for me to answer those questions. I prayed that they would forgive me for my honest answers.

I told my sons, "I had a drug problem, which took over my life and my mind. Even though I thought about you and loved you, the drugs were more important to me at the time. That was what the drugs were telling me. I left you with Grandma because I didn't want to drag you into my world of drugs and insanity, too. But you were always in my heart and in my thoughts."

I continued, "I was dealing with my own demons from my childhood. You did not have anything to do with that. And in no way did you do anything

wrong. I was the one that messed up. But what's important is that I'm here now and I love you guys to infinity and beyond."

## A Terrifying Moment

After my sons came home, it wasn't always easy to be a good mom. One afternoon I came home from work feeling very tired and found a message on my answering machine from JonPaul's teacher. She said JonPaul, who was 12, was not showing up to school. Plus, he had never turned in the $75 I gave him for his cap and gown.

I asked JonPaul, "What was that all about?" He was giving me all kinds of excuses, but when he said, "I don't care and I can do what I want," I just I totally lost it and started hitting on him. Almost without realizing what I was doing, I even grabbed him by his throat and started choking him.

He said, with tears in his eyes, "Mami, you're choking me." At that moment I saw myself in JonPaul and my mother in me. When I realized I was acting out the role of my mother, that scared the hell out of me. I panicked, let go and ran to the hallway where I sat on the steps and called my sister, sobbing.

When I calmed down, I hugged him and apologized and promised him that it would never happen again. After that, I recommitted myself to breaking my family's pattern. I made a conscious decision that I would talk to my boys no matter what they did that upset me, instead of treating them how my mother treated me.

## Listening to My Son

Since then, I haven't reacted so crazily to my children. I've realized that my son is still learning how to be a son and I am learning how to be a mother. Things got better one day at a time.

Another time I was very upset with him was when the teacher informed me that JonPaul had not turned in any homework for a whole week and disrespected her in front of the other students.

I felt the heat rising in my head. But by the time JonPaul got home, I had calmed down and thought out a strategy of how to approach him in a positive way. We talked and I really listened to what he had to say.

## We Pull Through

Today I have a good relationship with my boys. I communicate with them, something my mother and father never did with me. We share our thoughts and feelings, whether good or bad. We go out together and, every other weekend, we have family game night. We all sit around the table and play games like Parcheesi, Sorry, Charades and Operation.

At times, things get hectic, but we pull through. Like every teen and mom, we struggle together to understand one another. Together, we made a choice to break our family's pattern of violence and silence.

When I look back on what I've been through and what I put my kids through, I often start crying. Then I look at where I am today and realize I'm blessed. Not everyone gets a second chance.

## NOW LET'S TALK ABOUT THE STORY:

• How did adults in Milagros' family usually communicate with children?

• How did that pattern harm Milagros and her sons?

• What did Milagros' sons need to tell her? What did they need to hear from her?

• How did Milagros use visits to open up communication with her sons?

• At times, Milagros' first reaction is still to explode at her children. What helps her communicate calmly instead?

## PERSONAL REFLECTION TIME

Let's look at the worksheet called "My Reflections." Take 5 or 10 minutes to write down your answers on the worksheet and then we'll share. (*Wait until most people are finished.*)

• Who wants to share their responses?

## ENDING THE GROUP

Now turn to the "Visit Journal" worksheet. Take a few minutes to write down your goal for this week's visit. You can answer the "reflection" questions and fill in the checklist" after your visit. Please do that at home.

Next week, we'll start by talking about your visits. I look forward to hearing from everyone about how you tried to reach your goals!

## NEXT WEEK

Let's talk about how your visits went this week:
• Who tried to meet their goal? How did it go?
• Will someone share a moment they are proud of?
• Will someone talk about something they'd handle differently next time?

Thank you for sharing.

## My Reflections: Breaking a Painful Pattern by Milagros Sanchez

1. What do your children need to understand about why they're in foster care or what you are doing to reunite with them?

2. What concerns do you have about answering questions they may have for you?

3. What concerns do you have about asking your children questions about their experiences?

4. What might they need you to understand about their experiences in foster care?

## My Visit Journal – Breaking a Painful Pattern

**GOAL:** What is something—about their experiences in foster care or the steps you're taking to reunify with them—that you want to talk with your children about? Write down what you would like to say.

**REFLECTION:** Did you talk to your children as you'd planned to? How did it go?

What's something that you did to keep anger out of your visit that you feel proud of?

What is something you did to connect with your children?

OVER ⟶

## My Visit Journal Checklist: Breaking a Painful Pattern by Milagros Sanchez

Please use the checklist below to keep track of the steps you are taking to improve your visits. Use the "comments" section to make notes about your experiences.

| Did I... | Comments |
|---|---|
| ☐ Attend my visit | |
| ☐ Arrive on time | |
| ☐ Plan activities | |
| ☐ Bring toys | |
| ☐ Bring a snack | |
| ☐ Greet my child's foster parent | |
| ☐ Keep anger/frustration out of my visit | |
| ☐ Focus only on my child | |

Did I respond to my child's needs...

| | |
|---|---|
| ☐ for me to be trustworthy | |
| ☐ to follow a routine | |
| ☐ to have fun together | |
| ☐ to eat together | |
| ☐ to feel safe with the foster parent | |
| ☐ to talk about experiences in foster care | |
| ☐ to say goodbye in a positive way | |

# Words That Heal

*Sometimes it's hard to find the right words to say to your children. Here are some ways to communicate if you are having a hard time getting started. As you get comfortable talking about the difficult changes happening in your family, you will find your own words...*

"I am not sure yet when you can come home but I know I love you and I am doing everything I can."

"We will get to see each other here every _____."

"I really miss you and I want to help the foster parent take good care of you while you are away from me."

"It might be hard to talk about everything that is happening but I want to know how you are doing."

"It's OK if you don't want to talk to me, but please talk to someone about what you are thinking."

"I am really frustrated that we can't have overnight visits yet. I will call my social worker and talk to her about it later."

"If you have a problem with your foster parent, I can help you talk to them about it, but I don't want to get in the middle of the conflict."

"I know this is really hard but we will get through this."

"You seem really sad. Do you want to talk about anything?"

"You might have a lot of mixed up feelings these days. Do you have any questions?"

"I need to do some things before you can come home but none of this is your fault."

"I know you might be mad at me but you still need to listen and follow rules."

"I am sad to say goodbye to you too. I will see you in a few days and I'll be thinking of you all the time."

"I am talking to a counselor who is helping me and I'm doing OK. Don't worry about me."

*Adapted and reprinted with permission from* Family Connect: Putting the pieces of family visits together—a guide for parents. *Written by Wendy Negaard and published by Family Alternatives: www.familyalternatives.org*

# 'You Were Amazing!'

*Visit Coaches help parents bond with their children.*

By Lynne Miller

Last fall, I heard a presenter speak about a new program called Visit Coaching, which is designed to help families have better quality visits. I decided to sign up for the training to become a coach.

I know from experience how important visits are. My own son was in foster care. By coming early to visits and playing with him, I was able to show him that I loved him even though we were separated. Then, as a Parent Advocate at a foster care agency, I worked with parents to bond with their children during visits.

Visits can be stressful. When children are in foster care, visits can reflect all the pain, anger, confusion and fear that children and parents feel. Instead of being a time for families to come together and show their love, visits can feel awkward and upsetting.

Plus, visiting rooms at agencies are often over-crowded, and there aren't enough toys and games, so family members can become bored and fight. Sometimes kids wind up ignoring their parents to play with children from other families, or parents talk about their cases instead of playing with their children.

### Listening and Guiding

At the training sessions, I learned that the coach's role is to support parents in planning outings and dealing with kids' behavior. Coaches also accompany the family on visits to places like parks and playgrounds, libraries, or restaurants.

Coaches meet with the parents before and after each visit to talk to parents about their goals. Sometimes parents want help dealing with a child's behavior, like working on getting a child to greet the parent with a hug, or keeping kids from fighting with each other. Other times, parents want support planning outings, because parents may not have taken their children out much before their children were placed in foster care.

Most of all, I learned to listen to the parents, empathize, be nonjudgmental, and guide parents toward finding their own solutions to problems in their families.

### Help Saying 'No'

One mom I worked with was struggling with her kids' behavior because she just couldn't say no. Once we went to McDonald's and she bought each kid two sandwiches, fries, a milkshake and soda. Then the kids hardly ate anything. I could see by the look on her face that Mom was upset, but she rationalized it, saying, "Well, they can take it back to the foster home."

I just let the visit flow and talked afterward. I told her, "I know you feel guilty because your kids are in foster care, but you have to learn to say no."

"I know, but it's just so hard," she said. I explained that if she didn't set limits with her children now, she would have a harder time when they came home.

### Calm and Comfortable

Before each successive visit, I reminded Mom to be strong and have faith in herself. On a later visit, her kids were asking for everything under the sun. But she said no, and she was positive in the way she did it. She just said, "Not today," or, "Sorry, we can't afford that." Afterward, I patted her on the back and said, "You were amazing!"

I am so proud of this mom. One day, we all went to the park and she and the kids put on bathing suits and went in the sprinkler together. The mom had never done that before. The mom also went on the slide. She said to her kids, "I'm going to get stuck!" (she's a little chubby). But she got on with her kids pushing and pulling her, and she had fun. It was one of our best visits. She was calm and comfortable with her kids.

### Screaming Matches

Another family I worked with had communication issues. At first, the visits were screaming matches, usually between mom and daughter,

but sometimes also her son. I tried not to interfere but once I knew them better, I simply leaned over to the mom and whispered, "Gee, your daughter reminds me so much of you! I wonder if that's why you guys argue so much."

After the visit, Mom told me, "You know, in that moment I realized that my daughter and I were acting the way my mom and I act, and I decided it wasn't going to be that way between us. I have to learn to listen and let her speak—something my own mom wouldn't do."

Mom chose to start family therapy, which helped them to improve their communication. As time passed, I was so happy to see this mom sit and really listen to what her daughter had to say and respond with comments that let her daughter know that she'd heard her.

### The Skills to Succeed

Coaching other parents is difficult. In the first few visits, I had to find the patterns that were holding the family back from connection. I also had to control my own emotions and reactions. The first time I saw this mom and her daughter yelling at each other, it took a lot of self-control not to raise my voice, too! I had to remind myself: I am not here to boss anyone around. I am here to help Mom make the visit fun and to help them find answers for their family.

Some parents turn down Visit Coaching because they feel it's intrusive, but I believe the program can help many families. Visit Coaching helps parents plan and get support as they step back into their role as parents. It helps parents put their families on a path to reunification and success after foster care.

Rise

## My Achievements + Goals

Today is the last day of our group. Take some time to look back on your reflections and visit journals. Think about the steps you have taken to improve your visits and the steps you still want to take.

# MY ACHIEVEMENTS

1. At the beginning of the group, what were your goals?

2. What progress have you made in reaching your goals?

3. What is your proudest moment?

4. What did you learn from other parents in the group and what did you share that helped others?

5. Which story was most important to you and why?

## LOOKING BACK

Please describe what you think you learned about these topics:

• Thinking about your child's needs

• Arriving on time and being prepared

• Connecting with your child through shared activities

• Using routines to help your child feel safe

• Handling anger during visits

• Communicating with your child's foster parent

• Communicating with your child

Rise

## MY VISIT JOURNAL

**REFLECTION:** What is going well in your visits now?

**GOALS:** What are you going to keep working on?

1.

2.

3.

## MY SUPPORT TEAM

I can call on these group members, friends and family when I need support:

Name                              Phone Number                     Email

_____

_____

_____

_____

_____

_____

_____

_____

_____

_____

# Rise PARENTING RESOURCES
## *from RISE*

## *REUNIFICATION*
### *IT WON'T HAPPEN AGAIN*
Stories about reunification by parents
affected by the child welfare system

#CW-REUN, 82 pp. $12.00

When children act out after reunification, parents often feel
overwhelmed. Help parents understand children's fear and
anger and learn healthy responses that other parents have
used to repair relationships with their children.

• 9 stories by parents who have reunified with their children

• Discussion guides for each story—use in staff training,
parenting classes, or parent support groups

• Worksheets for each story to help parents reflect on their experiences and define "action
steps" they can take to handle the stresses of reunification

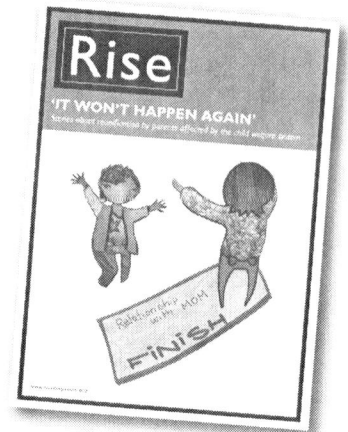

---

## *PARENTING SKILLS*
### *HEALING OURSELVES,*
### *HEALING OUR CHILDREN*
Stories about parenting by parents
affected by the child welfare system

#CW-HIST, 86 pp. $12.00

Parents who grew up with chaos, trauma, or family separation
need guidance to build safe, nurturing homes. Parents will feel
capable of setting routines, improving communication, and
using positive discipline when they read these stories by their
peers.

• 10 stories by child welfare-affected parents

• Discussion guides for each story—use in staff training, parenting classes, or support groups

• 2 interviews with child welfare experts

• Worksheets for each story to help parents reflect on their experiences and define "action
steps" they can take to strengthen their families

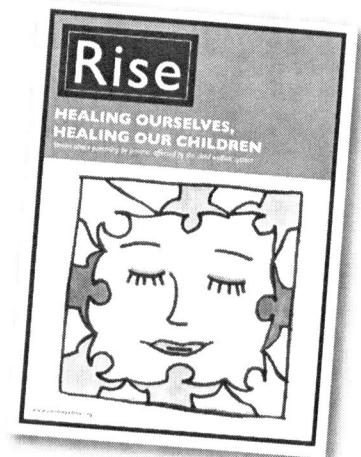

# PARENT-FOSTER PARENT RELATIONSHIPS

## *BUILDING A BRIDGE*

Stories about building collaboration
between parents and foster parents

#CW-BRD, 130 pp. $18.95

Positive relationships between parents and foster parents help children
feel more secure in care and adjust more easily after reunification.

*Building a Bridge* includes:

- 10 stories by parents
- 5 stories by foster parents
- 5 stories by teens
- 2 interviews with child welfare experts
- 14 Leader's Guides give you step-by-step instructions for using the stories in groups

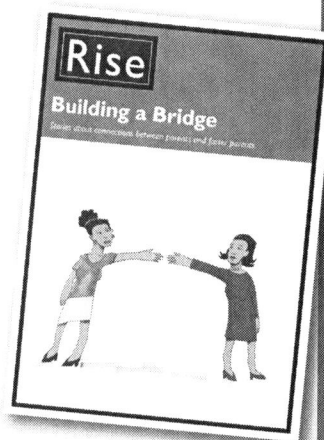

---

# FOUR EASY WAYS TO ORDER

**❶ Order Via the Web**
24 HOURS A DAY
www.risemagazine.org/
pages/resources.html

**❷ Fax Your Order**
24 HOURS A DAY
**212-279-8856**

**❸ Mail Your Order**
Rise/Youth Communication
224 W. 29th Street, 2nd floor
New York, NY 10001

**❹ Phone Your Order**
**212-279-0708**
x115

**Ship To: (No PO Boxes)**

Name_____

Title_____

Organization_____

Address_____

City_____State____Zip_____

Phone/e-mail_____

☐ Check Enclosed      ☐ Bill me (P.O. <u>must</u> be enclosed)
☐ Credit Card
Visa/Master Card    American Express    Discover (circle one)

Card #_____  Exp date_____

_____
Cardholder name exactly as it appears on card (please print)

_____
Cardholder Signature

**Healing Ourselves**

| | # of books | Total |
|---|---|---|
| 1-24 @ $12.00 each | _____ | ____ |
| 25-49 @ $11.00 each | _____ | ____ |
| 50 or more $10.00 each | _____ | ____ |

**It Won't Happen Again**

| | # of books | Total |
|---|---|---|
| 1-24 @ $12.00 each | _____ | ____ |
| 25-49 @ $11.00 each | _____ | ____ |
| 50 or more $10.00 each | _____ | ____ |

**Building a Bridge**

| | # of books | Total |
|---|---|---|
| 1-24 @ $18.95 each | _____ | ____ |
| 25-49 @ $16.95 each | _____ | ____ |
| 50 or more $12.95 each | _____ | ____ |

**Shipping & Handling**
$5 on orders up to $100
$10 on orders $101-$249
$15 on orders above $250

Shipping _____

Total _____

CPSIA information can be obtained at www.ICGtesting.com
Printed in the USA
BVOW040818270911

272214BV00003B/2/P